CALIFORNIA
DESIGN LIBRARY

KITCHENS

Diane Dorrans Saeks

CHRONICLE BOOKS

SAN FRANCISCO

For my son, Justin, with love, always. —D.D.S.

———————————————

Printed in Hong Kong

Book and Cover Design:
Madeleine Corson Design, San Francisco

Cover Photograph:
Kitchen design by Michael Berman, Los Angeles for Merrill Schindler.
Photograph by Grey Crawford, Los Angeles.

Title Page:
A kitchen by Santa Rosa designer Julie Atwood.
Photograph by Laurie E. Dickson.

Library of Congress Cataloging-in-Publication Data Available

ISBN 0-8118-1305-3

Distributed in Canada by:
Raincoast Books
8680 Cambie Street
Vancouver BC V6P 6M9

10 9 8 7 6 5 4 3 2

Chronicle Books
85 Second Street
San Francisco
California 94105

www.chroniclebooks.com

RECIPES FOR DELICIOUS KITCHENS

California kitchens are as varied, inspiring, and delicious as the food that's served forth in this bounteous state. The tasty kitchens of some of California's top interior designers, architects, and chefs are presented on these pages for inspiration. ⚲ California kitchens are comfortable, easy-going, and surprisingly traditional in style. While you might expect Californians to be experimental and willing to leap on the newest trends, most opt for familiar styles with a twist. ⚲ Berkeley chef Alice Waters's kitchen has a big bay window, a brick fireplace, and a large copper sink that glints and gleams at her as she rinses fragrant herbs and vegetables fresh from her garden. Napa Valley chef Thomas Keller, owner of The French Laundry, loves classical music playing on the stereo, fresh flowers, baskets of farm vegetables, a good stock of extra-virgin olive oils, and Champagne chilling in the refrigerator. Oakland chef Paul Bertolli, co-owner of Oliveto, likes to have a fireplace for grilling, his own home-brewed balsamic vinegars, and a view of vegetables flourishing in his garden. ⚲ Once kitchens were afterthoughts, laboratories, or drab and unfulfilling utilitarian corners hidden below stairs. Today they are the most used, enjoyed, and lived-in part of a house or apartment. ⚲ Kitchens today must be much more than just a place for cooking. Now they are action-central — the hub of the house. They have to perform well as an arena for preparing, cooking, and enjoying meals; as a family room; and as an inviting place for socializing. They should also provide efficient and decorative storage. Ideally they will accomplish it all with style. ⚲ That's why billions of dollars are spent every year updating and improving old kitchens. Even a kitchen that was remodeled ten or fifteen years ago is probably very outdated with unfashionable appliances and colors, and an unworkable, time-wasting layout. ⚲ In this book, you will find hundreds of style ideas and practical recommendations as well as provocative opinions from trend-setting chefs and architects. You'll also notice that the emphasis here is on designing a kitchen to suit your needs — not for the resale value or to follow design trends, and especially not to impress others. Many of the pleasures of a truly satisfying kitchen are spelled out here, and you're encouraged to dream, imagine, and open your mind to new possibilities for your kitchen. Rather than letting name-brand appliances or plastic laminate counters dictate how your kitchen will look and feel, visualize something more poetic and elusive. Enjoy a reverie of old copper pots, a chair by the fireside, pristine white porcelain sinks, a brass faucet salvaged from an old building. Other worthy goals for starters include winter sunshine, silence, room for children to read at the counter while parents prepare dinner, a view of trees, quick access to a patio, and French doors to the garden. Berkeley building/architecture guru Christopher Alexander notes in his influential book, *A Pattern Language,* that the kitchen needs the sun more than other rooms, not less. "Plan the main part of the kitchen counter on the south and southeast side of the kitchen, with big windows around it, so that sun can flood in and fill the kitchen with yellow light both morning and afternoon," he suggests. Materials should be friendly, perhaps custom-crafted or -finished, and even in quirky colors. ☿ "The trend now in remodeling kitchens is to combine great function and an efficient layout with warm, friendly materials," advises San Francisco architect Dan Phipps, who has renovated hundreds of kitchens since he started his practice thirteen years ago. "While some people still like a hard-edged, streamlined super-efficient look, today most homeowners want timeless, classic design with a congenial traditional feeling," Phipps says. "Kitchens should first of all suit the specific needs and style of the owners. They shouldn't look like a factory." ☿ There is no one perfect recipe for all California kitchens. Some of the chefs and designers I consulted like wood-burning ovens, armchairs, and sound systems, while others swear by granite-topped worktables, white walls, gleaming floors, and esoteric equipment. Assembled on these pages are all the essential ingredients of fine kitchen design. ☿ These reports, notes, pointers, meditations, tips on good kitchen design, and tales from the war zone of remodeling are highly opinionated. Even the experts I've assembled here don't agree. Some like romantic lights, others prefer efficient high-tech lighting systems. ☿ Our experts help you plot a workable plan, avoid mistakes, and achieve a kitchen that's practical and personal. ☿ When your kitchen projects are complete, take out a cookbook and prepare your favorite dishes. As the fragrance of baking and grilling fills your kitchen, see how much you love cooking. ☿ That's the true test of a great kitchen. ☿ Bon appetit! PAGE 6 Designer Julie Atwood placed a handsome worktable in the center of this friendly California kitchen. OPPOSITE Bold strokes and perfect symmetry give this San Francisco kitchen timeless style. Design: Neos.

STYLE PORTFOLIO

How are efficient, warm, comfortable, friendly, and timeless kitchens designed? What do interior designers, architects, and kitchen designers know that non-professionals can learn? How do designers get their kitchens to look just-so? On the following pages I present the pick of the crop of tasty California kitchens. I selected the broadest range—from neat and simple to jam-packed and wonderfully overflowing with great things. Clearly, a great variety of kitchens work well, and quirky, individual style is always the most satisfying. While some kitchen renovators obsess over every teeny detail, it's always important to keep the big picture in view. The most successful designs are cohesive. Each designer rejects theme design— something more personal always works best. The proof is in the pudding.

OPPOSITE Architectural designer John Davis's shipshape kitchen in Stinson Beach.

Barbara Barry is a polymath. As she goes from one design project and achievement to another, from one airport or country to the next, her inspiration and ideas and drawings keep springing up. In just a few fast years, Barry has limned interiors, furniture, lighting, linens, tabletop decor, carpets, fabric for office and home, and rather splendid new tableware. ♀ When, you might ask, is she at home and when does she ever have time to enjoy her handsome white-and-green kitchen? "Time at home is sweet and meaningful because my work is intense and demanding and takes me all over the country," said Barry. "When I do finally have a Saturday morning at home, after a business trip to New York or Hawaii or Chicago, I'm ecstatic." ♀ Barry dances to the muted music of white. For her, the infinite range of whites is pure beauty — soothing, timeless, classic, and always tasty and refreshing. She also loves a wide range of green colors but uses them sparingly. ♀ "I'm inspired by all the greens in nature, from pond scum to celadon, Chinese cabbages, spring leaves, moss, bamboo, and grass," she said. "I never tire of green." In fact, the walls are painted acid/apple green, which Barry mixed on site. Color is also used to ground the room and keep the scheme from floating away. The floor of quartersawn oak is stained a medium fruitwood tone. ♀ Barbara Barry believes that a kitchen should be furnished not like a laboratory but like a room. "I like to furnish a kitchen with a good, solid table and some chairs, along with banks of cabinets and drawers," she said. "I like the idea of an étagère for holding books, an old bookcase to hold cookbooks, photography and collections, and perhaps old cabinets." ♀ She likes to carve out extra counter space or position a table so that she can mount tablescapes of platters, and bowls and trays of seasonal fruit and vegetables. ♀ "I have a lamp for lighting, rather than just an overhead light," said Barry. "An overhead light can be harsh and glary. You set the lamp where you need it, for reading, cooking, dining. It brings the room down to a more intimate scale."

OPPOSITE & ABOVE Barbara Barry's kitchen counters are honed white marble. She likes the satiny matte texture honing accomplishes. The cabinets and fixtures, painted linen white, are all new but were designed to appear original to the house. For this designer, white is never plain vanilla. Cabinets are painted a chic linen white and the Italian tiles are milky white.

When entrepreneur/political activist Susie Buell renovated and remodeled her kitchen, she took a very practical approach — one that has lots of style and family friendly nooks and crannies. Light and air and a sense of space were there aplenty in the apartment overlooking the San Francisco Bay. ⚲ The kitchen, which faces east, has two large windows overlooking the city. When they're open and sounds of the streets below drift in, the apartment feels connected to the bustle but very much above it all in its coziness. The adjoining dining room and breakfast room have buckets of sunlight. ⚲ The "bones" were fine. Susie, who co-founded Esprit, is a practical woman, and she planned no major changes. She simply wanted to reconfigure the kitchen to maximize countertops, work space, and shelves for displaying her collection of green glass and ceramics. ⚲ Susie was also experienced and savvy enough about design to know that the best approach here — as in many renovations — would be to respect the existing architecture and ethos. A "modern" kitchen and an attempt to impose a 1996 kitchen style on a twenties building would have been jarring and inappropriate. ⚲ Adjoining pantries and cabinets offer plenty of storage without imposing on the low-key nature of the kitchen. The new floor plan is simple and direct. Cabinets, shelves, and new woodwork were kept very understated and traditional in tone so that they would seem to have been those originally installed. ⚲ Susie, her daughters, and chums bring baskets full of fruit, fresh pastas, honey, eggs, and vegetables in from the Saturday farmers' market at the downtown Ferry Plaza. Nothing gives this family more summer pleasure than unloading their market bounty, tasting the fresh vegetables and fruit, and using them to make luncheon salads and vegetable frittatas, or

stashing them in the refrigerator. Friends gather around the counters. ⚲ The kitchen is also just the right size for a large dinner party or for two people reading the Sunday paper, making toast, and sipping coffee in the morning sunlight. Perhaps best of all, this is one design that will not become dated — and the happy residents will never tire of it.

OPPOSITE & ABOVE White walls and white-painted cabinets provide the perfect background for Susie's ever-growing collection of green objects, from glass plates and cups to thirties glasses, travel souvenirs, and flea market treasures. The *pique-assiette* vase filled with sunflowers from the farmers' market is a tribute to Susie's Jack Russell terrier, Gracie.

Over the past fifteen years, interior designer Candra Scott has crafted a very successful career in historic restoration. Among her portfolio of successes are the new Hotel Rex in downtown San Francisco and the Hotel Boheme in San Francisco's beatific North Beach. ☿ With each hotel, Scott has turned back the clock. Using a combination of sleight-of-hand, authentic antiques, and pure invention, she has taken time-worn interiors and turned them into jazzy riffs on vintage style and bygone happy times. ☿ When the moment came to turn her attention to her own house, a 1904 Edwardian on a sunny hillside just south of downtown, she took the same highly detailed, multi-layered, patient approach. ☿ "I specialize in creating new interiors that look as if they have been there forever and are historically correct," she said. "I research and reinvent everything, from wall finishes and ceilings to lamps, accessories, floors, and furniture." ☿ Her kitchen had been what she described as a "lumber-yard quickie," put in by the previous owner to help sell the house. Despising the cheap wood and "heartless" laminates, Scott removed everything down to the bare walls. ☿ Her new cabinets, with red-lacquered mullions inspired by Chinese screens, were crafted

by Jim Sellars. ☿ Candra Scott's kitchen is pure invention. "I like to start with a history of the house and build a little design fiction around it," she said. "I imagined that the homeowners remodeled in the thirties and built the first real kitchen then," she said. "This cream, apple green, and red color scheme was all the rage."

☿ "I wasn't aiming for museum-like authenticity or a real, slavish period piece," she said. "I call it 'Kitchen Chinois' — thirties with a hint of Chinese influence." For inspiration, Scott viewed films like *Indochine, Farewell My Concubine,* and *The Lover,* set in China and Indochina early in the century. ☿ "I look for subtle details," she said. "Then I translate those, using poetic license." ☿ Scott has authentic thirties and forties equipment, including a Mixmaster, a waffle iron, a pressure cooker, and art vases. She does not have a dishwasher. "If it did not exist in the thirties, I don't have it," she said with satisfaction.

OPPOSITE & ABOVE Scott designed a colorful new floor using red, yellow, and green Armstrong tiles. She cut 12-inch-by-12-inch tiles down to 6 inches by 6 inches for better scale. In the center is an original 1930s linoleum "rug." The painted table and chairs, circa 1925, were found in New York. The tablecloths and kitchen linens are part of her collection of vintage textiles. The walls are painted a rich egg-cream color. Scott's inspiration: Brass mesh inset into cabinet doors both conceals and reveals the contents.

Photographer/interior designer David Livingston recently completed a remodel of the kitchen in his house in the Marin County hills just north of San Francisco. ⚥ The ranch-style house had begun life in the sixties, and the kitchen was boring and basic. Cooking then was a non-event, said Livingston. Mid-century homeowners were satisfied with their kitchens as long as they had a window over the sink so they could daydream as they sudsed the dishes. ⚥ The original kitchen had a very standard U-shaped layout. Livingston wanted a new kitchen that would be at once a workshop, a cocktail lounge, and a cooking facility. He reconfigured the floor plan and converted it to a wide galley, with improved storage, a skylight, a door leading to the garden, and new appliances. ⚥ "I cook a lot, so I wanted a stove with gas burners that would be hot and easy to clean," said the designer. "The oven is opposite, beside a counter. I use it every day." ⚥ The designer planned a work side and a storage side. The sink, Russell cooktop, dishwasher, and marble prep counter are grouped together. Opposite is a wall of compact storage that organizes everything from hardware to garden shears, spices, candles, napkins, cups. In the

handsome stretch of cabinetry is a counter where Livingston and friends can gather for coffee or a glass of wine. ⚥ "Now I love coming home after foraging at the Marin County farmers' market," Livingston said. "For a couple of hours, I slice and dice, stocking the kitchen with my new creations. This, for me, is the joy of my new kitchen." ⚥ Livingston opened up the ceiling with a skylight that pours light into the small room during the day. A glass door, which opens to the hillside garden, also brings light into the room. Joining those who love wood floors (some cooks do not) the designer chose

cost-effective Australian spotted gum. The bold patterning and roseate tones of the timber are particularly pleasing in this small space. Another clever move — shown in the photograph opposite — was to leave one side of the kitchen open to a hallway and display/storage wall. The open shelves in this lit niche appear to be part of the kitchen.

OPPOSITE & ABOVE Shipshape and fancy-free: David Livingston's reinvented kitchen is just 10 feet by 13 feet, so every inch counted in this renovation. With his redesign, the dishwasher is placed high for easier access. The sink is adjacent to the Russell cooktop so that hot pans can get a fast flash of water, making cleaning easier. Opposite the work counter, a display niche gathers the appliances, stores bowls, and provides an "altar" for ripe fruit and other treasures from the farmers' markets. The Fieldstone cabinets are in cherry and maple.

KEN HOM

A KITCHEN IN BERKELEY

Restaurateur/best-selling cookbook author/television celebrity and international bon vivant Ken Hom has homes in London, Paris, and the south of France. But it's in Berkeley that he has this handsome, hardworking kitchen. In fact, the 18-foot-by-18-foot kitchen takes up half of the downstairs floor of his house. ⚲ When he began the renovation, Hom was extremely pragmatic. "I wanted everything to be open and visible so that I wouldn't have to go hunting," he said. "I work fast and like to have everything in reach. Ingredients and equipment should all be out there. To me, there is no sense in trying to hide them." ⚲ Hom doesn't like to have a large refrigerator because he uses most ingredients very fresh. He has a restaurant wok-burner, a Wolf range, and a heavy-duty dishwasher. ⚲ "I decided to spend money on equipment, not expensive cabinetry," said Hom. "And though I would have liked butcherblock counters because I like the natural look, my contractor said I might have problems with wear and tear. I agreed to put in Formica. I'm glad I did because it's very long-lasting, practical, and easy to clean." ⚲ Hom chose dark-red countertops because, he said, food looks good on it. ⚲ "I've put in a sealed terra-cotta paver floor, which adds warmth and character to the kitchen," said Hom. "I thought about wooden floors because I like the look of them, but they need care, and if you splash water or drop something they can get slippery." ⚲ Hom surmised that he would continue improving his kitchen. "I've just added an extra phone line," he said. "And I'm putting in more electric plugs near the sink. These are small things that make a big difference." ⚲ This is, of course, the kitchen of a man whose life is cooking. Still, Hom's approach can be bitten off in small chunks or served in smaller portions. ⚲ Most of all, Ken Hom believes in function over style in kitchens.

Perhaps his best suggestion is that a kitchen should be allowed to evolve and improve over time. ⚲ "Every now and then, look and see that you are still using every corner of the kitchen, and consider changing storage. Perhaps you have changed the kind of cooking you do — the kitchen should reflect new needs."

OPPOSITE Ken Hom, who presents popular television shows on cooking in Great Britain and France, keeps ingredients for French, Italian, Chinese — and American — cooking in his Northern California kitchen. "I don't seem to be able to group them — I'm not that organized," he joked. "I know where everything is, even if I don't have all the oils or vinegars in one place." ABOVE Ken Hom's *batterie de cuisine* is impressive. Hom believes in function over style. "Always think about practicality before looks or style or what others may think," he advised. "And let the kitchen change and improve over time."

When award-winning pastry chef and best-selling cookbook author Emily Luchetti is not away on a book tour or traveling to China with her husband, Peter, she loves to be in her kitchen cooking. ⚲ "At home, cooking is pure pleasure, great enjoyment," said Luchetti. A native of New York State, she is a graduate of the New York Restaurant School. She was formerly the pastry chef at Stars restaurant in San Francisco, and has been named one of the top ten pastry chefs by *Chocolatier* magazine. ⚲ "It was important to me to have a great view of the Bay," said Luchetti. "Since I knew I'd be cooking a lot in the kitchen, I felt I deserved a view. It would be horrible to have the kitchen stuck in the back of the house with views only from the living room." ⚲ Luchetti is truly at home in this kitchen. That's partly because she is a natural, brilliant cook, but also because she's working in a kitchen designed specifically for her needs. ⚲ The house is nestled in a green hillside in Sausalito with a view across Richardson Bay, dotted with yachts, sculls, houseboats, seals, flying boats, and other fascinating flotsam. ⚲ The Luchettis' house, as shipshape and streamlined as one of the vessels that ply San Francisco Bay, was designed nine years ago by Peter's brother Robert, a noted architect. His offices are in Cambridge, Massachusetts. ⚲ The 20-foot-by-12-foot kitchen, sculptural and cohesive, has a dining area, two small pantries, beautiful surfaces, and one of the best views in the house. Its floor is set two steps higher than the two-story living room to give it a grandstand viewing position. ⚲ In one pantry, Emily keeps all of the artistic plates she collects. In the other are her microwave oven, specialized preparation counters, and—since it's used mainly for long-term storage—the freezer. The refrigerator (without a freezer compartment) is in the kitchen. An ice machine in the "bar area" saves trips back to the pantry freezer for ice. It's all as efficient and well planned as a professional kitchen. ⚲ The icing on the cake is that while the chef got her wish for a work space that meets very specific needs, this is truly a two-person kitchen and Peter often cooks with Emily.

OPPOSITE & ABOVE Emily Luchetti's Sausalito kitchen strikes the perfect balance between smooth styling with luxurious materials and pure practicality. The custom-designed kitchen has the kind of materials, colors, style, and equipment that will not date. Luchetti was not interested in anything trendy. She favors easy-to-maintain stainless steel, low-luster mahogany, and large areas of marble. Equipment includes Gaggenau wall ovens, range, dishwasher, and a pro-sized Sub-Zero refrigerator.

The white-walled kitchen in costume designer Theadora Van Runkle's quiet cottage could be called "Metamorphosis." ⚲ In the sixties, it was dark brown; in the seventies, it looked very Arts & Crafts; in the eighties, Victorian. A handful of years ago, she replaced a tan "Sears Special" with a shining white forties stove, and brought in a *faux-marbre*-topped bow-front credenza. She painted the walls gleaming white, painted the floor matte white, and brought in all-white collections of dinnerware. Cake stands of cut glass play a walk-on role. ⚲ It's a romantic kitchen that also works well. There's plenty of counter space for preparing breakfast and room for making coffee, a lavish duck dinner for six, or a fortifying afternoon tea for her Sunday sketch club. ⚲ Fretwork shelves on the wall hold tins of exotic teas and coffees and a selection of white coffeepots and jams. ⚲ "I found that what-not at an antiques shop in Santa Monica and brought it home because it looked awkwardly endearing — like something made in a woodworking class," said Van Runkle, who painted the three-tiered shelf white. ⚲ On a higher shelf, she stores pots and pans, pressed-glass collections, vintage tea canisters, and picnic baskets.

⚲ Van Runkle installed her white microwave on Victorian brackets. ⚲ "I probably broke all sorts of kitchen planning rules, but it works wonderfully for me," said the designer, who is revered for her costumes for *Bonnie and Clyde, Myra Breckinridge*, and Coppola's *Godfather* films. "Often the best and most memorable design has 'flaws.' It's always the unexpected that captures your imagination, not something that was done absolutely by the book and is completely soulless." ⚲ She did not have to go far from her Laurel Canyon house to find an old stove. Los Angeles has several stores that specialize in restoring functional old designs. ⚲ Van Runkle treasures time at home, surrounded by her cats, Hazel and Charlotte, and a verdant fern-filled garden. "I leave the French doors open as the morning sun comes in, and I make a cup of tea and read scripts and dream," she said. "I feel very blessed."

OPPOSITE Kitchen style: Theadora Van Runkle installed a Victorian credenza in which she keeps silverware, plates, and large bowls. She painted the *faux marbre* top herself. Making imaginative use of wall space, she installed a wide shelf near the ceiling. The kitchen is perfect for the designer and a guest or two, and easily accommodates her eight-member Sunday sketch club.
ABOVE This is where friends linger with Earl Grey loose-leaf tea and Cyclamen Studio cups at hand.

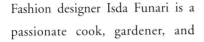

Fashion designer Isda Funari is a passionate cook, gardener, and entertainer. With a rich family background that includes Sicilian and Mexican grandparents, and with two decades of far-flung travel to her credit, she brings a worldly sensibility to both her clothing and kitchen design. ☿ In a sunny clearing beside her renovated log house in the Santa Cruz Mountains, she grows a summer bounty of tomatoes and zucchini. All summer long she carries in fresh herbs and armfuls of her favorite spicy green basil. Isda is known for her pungent pesto. ☿ The house shelters beneath redwoods. Roses climb over the fence, and zinnias bob in the breeze. It's an idyllic setting — blissful most of the year but occasionally dark and rainy in the winter months. Originally built as a summer residence, the house was "one step away from being a tent" when Funari and her beau, contractor Tony Melendrez, discovered it nine years ago. It had no insulation and few modern amenities, but it was full of potential. The couple patiently and thoughtfully remodeled it, staying true to its rustic spirit and aesthetic. ☿ To do justice to her growing and cooking, Funari and Melendrez designed and crafted a handsome, hardworking new kitchen, though it looks as if it has always been there. Melendrez used hefty materials and crafted them in a straightforward and bold manner. This is a kitchen that belongs to the house; it feels at home within its framework. ☿ The kitchen was carved out of two dim, poky rooms with tiny windows. Today, a bank of windows opens walls to the sunlight and forest views, and handsome, glossy white cabinets provide storage. Thick butcherblock counters were built-in to add warmth and reassuring substance to serious work areas. The massive island gives everyone — Isda and

Tony and helpful friends — plenty of work space. And all around, hefty pots and pans and bowls are just a step or two away. ☿ It's reassuring and visually pleasing to have cooking essentials lined up ready for action, too. Dinner can be improvised with dried herbs from the garden, flour, beans, and spices in glass jars.

OPPOSITE & ABOVE Serious fun: In Isda Funari and Tony Melendrez's kitchen, the neutral color scheme makes way for the sculptural counters, heavy-duty equipment, and mounds of vegetables from the garden. Funari's handpicked treasures from travel around the world include white ironstone, framed cigarette-card graphics, baskets, textiles, and antique glasses. The lantern is practical as well as necessary. Here in the giant redwoods of the Santa Cruz Mountains, fierce winter storms chase summer's sweet serenity, and the power may be out for hours.

Take inspiration from highly respected interior designer Ann Jones, who urges confidence when facing a dull apartment kitchen. Think of a basic rented kitchen as merely a starting point — not the room you must tolerate come what may. ⚲ "Many people think they can't make any changes — that they can't touch anything at all — when they are renting an apartment or house," she notes. "In fact, if you really dislike the kitchen tiles, hate the wallpaper, and can't live with the paint of the cabinets, you should talk to your landlord about changing them," she recommended. "While you might not want to go to the expense of major alterations, new kitchen flooring you install yourself and a quick coat of paint on walls or cabinets can be negotiated with your landlord. He or she will probably not mind if you make improvements, and perhaps change the floor from dull gray or hideous green to smart black and white or a stone-beige color." ⚲ Jones said a few swift moves can give cheer to a stodgy room. Semigloss white wall paint can unify a mismatched or cluttered design. Simply installed shelves can make a dated kitchen feel like home — and the shelves can easily be disassembled when you depart. Restaurant supply houses can be an inexpensive source for metal shelving, steel-topped storage units, and ultra-hard-wearing equipment. ⚲ Design can also be a mix of new and old. Antique furniture such as an old dining table, quirky flea market chairs, or an oversized, carved storage cabinet will also give an interim kitchen a bolder, friendlier feeling. "An old chest or dresser can provide storage for linens and dinnerware, and odds and ends that are not used every day," she said. "You might be lucky enough to have one fine piece of inherited furniture, but you could easily improvise with a junk store find and an

afternoon paint job. Paint the cabinet interiors a contrast just for fun." ⚲ Jones restyled her own drab Pacific Heights kitchen to make it chic and efficient. "We didn't remodel, just sort of refaced," said Jones. "We painted the existing cabinets gray, and changed the countertops from unattractive tiles to granite-like laminate."

OPPOSITE & ABOVE In the formerly rather dull kitchen of her Pacific Heights apartment, San Francisco interior designer Ann Jones uses silver trophies — found at flea markets — to hold antique silver cutlery. (The elaborately engraved tributes to forgotten winners of long-ago contests in obscure sports are part of the fun.) The kitchen gained style — and reasons for lingering — with framed posters, new laminate countertops, vintage furniture, and colorful flowers. A wall shelf in the hall beside the kitchen door offers extra storage — and a useful surface for utensils and a chiller when Ann and her husband entertain.

DESIGN WORKBOOK

Remodeling is exciting and requires all your attention and enthusiasm.
Listen to the experts' advice on these pages before taking the first step.
Check out the range of prices of every element in your kitchen — from
tiles to granite to cabinet doors and faucets. There are many ways of
using unexpected materials to keep costs down. Many remodelers today
visit salvage yards, flea markets, and demolition companies for vintage
and antique fixtures, old stoves, handsome sinks. If you want top-of-the-
line European cabinetry with high-tech finishes that knock your socks
off, you will pay more than for the plain oak cabinets from the lumber-
yard or cabinetmaker in your neighborhood. Restaurant-quality appliances are more expensive, but they're built to last. Be a smart renovator.
If something does not look right, don't dither. Speak to the contractor.

OPPOSITE In Helie Robertson's San Anselmo kitchen: a working vintage stove.

KITCHEN AID

**California's best architects and designers offer expert advice.
And always remember: God is in the details.**

You love your house. You love your neighborhood. But you don't love your kitchen. Maybe all it needs is a quick fix—a wash of paint on the cabinets or a dash of style on the counter. But maybe it's simply not working, and termites are feasting on your rafters. It's definitely time to consider remodeling. Today, there's a new style-conscious, more conservative approach to renovation. Instead of the glitzy and grandiose block-buster redesigns of the eighties, the pros today recommend a kitchen remodel that's subtle, practical, timeless, and in keeping with the style and scale of the house.

The most successful remodels often begin with a promising but down-in-the-dumps house, and carefully turn a so-so kitchen into a splendid one. The sensitively revised room feels as if it belongs to the house. The reconfigured floor plan works, it's more comfortable, and the house design looks seamless and all-of-a-piece. Nothing looks tacked on, trendy, or out of place. The kitchen is at home in the house.

Learn from pros with successful renovation stories. Start, as they all did, with a well-conceived overall plan and a strong personal vision. Study all the local building codes if you're doing it yourself. As designer Julie Atwood suggests, avail yourself of all the free advice you can find—from hardware stores, libraries, design books, and builders' supply companies. And if you plan a slow do-it-yourself project, consider hiring an architect or designer on a single-fee, one-time basis. Experience counts. Expert advice can only improve your design.

According to Emeryville, Northern California, architect Henry Siegel, for most homeowners, remodeling a kitchen often takes much more time and money than you might think. Expect from two to four months of construction for a kitchen renovation, depending on the scope and materials. Plan for six to nine months for a top-to-bottom remodel. Estimate from $30,000 and up for a newly designed kitchen, depending on the materials chosen. (For a top-to-bottom house remodel, the cost will be at least $100 per square foot in California.)

Before you've even started the reconstruction, the process of finding and hiring your architect or designer, designing the renovation, getting bids, checking references, and getting permits to remodel can take up to six months.

Think carefully before buying an old house. Remodeling is a serious business. "First you have to destroy old construction or cut a swathe through plaster or a brick wall to begin repair and the remodel," said Siegel. "Concealed substandard or inadequate construction, dry rot, or termite damage can

A B O V E Everything is at hand in Thomas Heinser and Madeleine Corson's South of Market kitchen. Note stainless steel counters.

O P P O S I T E Three walls of windows in this Napa Valley kitchen keep the room sparkling all year. Frame-and-panel cabinets in two tones of cherry mimic the Craftsman style in a new house. Kitchen designed by Nancy Lind Cooper. White Corian counters, granite bar.

cause delays and unexpected expense. There will be surprises."

It's tempting to do some of the work yourself, but seasoned renovators say it is often best to find professionals you can afford — they may save you money and time in the long run. The result will probably be more cohesive, aesthetic, and "polished." And choose top-quality materials for your renovation whenever possible. Renovating is expensive and time consuming, and you probably won't want to have to do it again in five years because the kitchen cabinets didn't hold up.

Remember, there's no one special formula for a remodel. Formulate the big picture. Get a plan. Just don't do it piecemeal or the result will be spotty. Choose the perfect style of finishes and materials in your price range. Work as a team with your designer, contractor, and craftspeople. Pay attention to details, and the finished kitchen will be pure pleasure.

OPPOSITE Terrence O'Flaherty's Telegraph Hill kitchen boasts marble counters, tall windows, a linen-upholstered banquette.

BELOW Santa Rosa designer Julie Atwood selected hearty materials and a wide-open plan for her own country house kitchen.

GETTING STARTED WITH KITCHEN DESIGN

Time for some fresh thinking on kitchens. Get rid of the old clichés with help from a leading California kitchen designer.

Steven J. Livingston of Snaidero Kitchens and Design in San Francisco has had years of experience designing custom kitchens. Born in Scotland, he trained in design in London and settled in San Francisco in 1989. He established the first independent Snaidero European kitchen studio in the U.S. in San Francisco and recently opened a second showroom in Palo Alto.

Livingston believes that kitchen design is a precise and exacting task — requiring the full attention and creativity of the designer, the contractor, craftspeople, and the homeowner. But he also avers that the process should be as much fun as cooking your favorite dish — and the result as delicious.

These are his useful insights into the design process, developing your design, and keys to a successful kitchen.

Don't Worry About Resale Value. Obsessing about which design or material will have the best resale value can only create an impersonal design lacking charm, hands-on care, and individuality. Assuming that you will be living in the house or apartment for five years or more, you should make your own enjoyment a top priority. Don't worry about what the next person — your buyer — will be thinking or what value they might place on your style. If you plan to live in the house for at least ten years, assume that the next owner will most likely remodel it to their liking anyway. They'll at least want to update appliances, paint walls, and refinish or refresh cabinet fronts. Unless you go overboard with a kitchen that is wildly one-of-a-kind and customized to your every whim, potential buyers will appreciate a stylish kitchen and

prefer it to a bland white box or a model-home, tried-and-true, bland design.

Be True to Your Own Taste. Clip pages from design magazines to develop your eye. The kitchen should be a reflection of the owner. It should be appropriate to the architecture, age, style, and location of the house. The more thought you give the design, the less standard or "stock" it will be. Try to identify ideas, colors, materials, and equipment that give you great pleasure. Once you've identified your style and direction, stay focused on that direction so that you won't

end up with a hodge-podge of styles. You can incorporate several strong elements as long as they work together to create harmony in the overall project.

Be Adventurous. If you like color, use it. Consider using more than one color on cabinets. (All one color can be monotonous.) Consider contrasting colors for splash or tiles or floor, rather than having everything match. Explore unexpected materials beyond granite

ABOVE Graphic designer Tom Bonauro has the perfect one-person kitchen that welcomes his favorite feline.

OPPOSITE Large-scale overhead beams, a cross-hatched concrete floor, and copper lighting give this kitchen personality.

countertops and wood cabinets. Bright lacquered furniture may be your style. Also consider easy-to-maintain concrete countertops, a solid-glass or brushed and lacquered stainless steel splash. Many of these more imaginative materials are less expensive than standard models — which can free up your budget to spend more on appliances or cabinets.

Don't Be Intimidated by Rules. Break out of the "working triangle" floor plan. Make your plan comfortable to move from the refrigerator to the cooktop and to the sink. Then it will work for you. Take the structure of the room into account. Plan ample countertop and storage space. (Plan more storage than you think you need — it will inevitably fill up.)

Focus on Your Objectives and Requirements. The final kitchen plan and style should enhance your life. If you entertain often, ensure that guests and family will gravitate to the kitchen by providing counterspace and chairs or stools for them. If you're an occasional cook, go lighter on the gadgets and appliances and direct more of the budget to countertops, comfort, and style.

Arm Yourself with Information. Investigate materials and other options so that you can make informed choices. Visit showrooms and gather brochures. Start a notebook with paint chips, tiles, prices, resources. Talk to your friends who have gone through a remodel. By visiting lumber yards, stores like Home Depot, kitchen supply stores, and hardware stores, as well as top-quality kitchen showrooms, you gain a solid knowledge and a realistic picture.

Don't Select Tiny Finishing Details First. Look at the big picture. Start with major items and work down. Cabinetry will probably be the big-budget item —

unless you're doing major structural work — so choose that early.

Don't Be Too Frugal. You'll be living with your kitchen and selections for a long time. Economize where it's less noticeable. Basic cabinet interiors may free up money for more-striking doors. If you really want the best gas range, and you'll use it often, find a way of figuring it into the budget. Another design element could be simplified. Check out the range of prices of every element in your kitchen — from tiles to granite to cabinet doors and faucets. For top quality, you will pay more. There are many ways of using unexpected materials to keep costs down, or doing without a greenhouse window. There is no such thing as a kitchen bargain — if you want top-of-the-line European cabinetry with high-tech finishes that knock your socks off, you will pay more than for the plain oak cabinets from the lumberyard or cabinetmaker in your neighborhood. Restaurant-quality appliances are more expensive, but they're built to last.

Get a Written Time Line from Your Contractor. The general contractor will schedule the various trades and keep them on schedule. Be sure that everyone is communicating, responsible, and available.

ABOVE Vintage fabrics, chequered floor, whimsical lighting are pure charm.

OPPOSITE Helie Robertson's San Anselmo kitchen feels like the archetypal gathering place with its massive table and beautiful light.

Architect Henry Siegel and his wife, attorney Kyra Subbotin, bought a charming and unpretentious 1907 Craftsman-style house on a tree-lined street in Elmwood, east of San Francisco.

The old floor plan seemed downright dumb, he said, chopping the house into a series of small rooms. The kitchen was a gloomy afterthought between the laundry and a poky pantry. They dreamed of better things. Ten tenacious months later, their new bungalow sports new shingles, a new roof, an updated and enlarged kitchen, and sunny new

rooms. Clearly the very best renovators are nothing but optimistic.

"The house had integrity," said Siegel. "I wanted to maintain the Craftsman style with a 'quiet' renovation. It's important to respect, not reject, the original architecture and the way it's detailed."

Siegel does not admire renovations that look as if they flew in from another neighborhood. Still, he didn't go overboard with a slavish line-for-line restoration. "A period kitchen can make you feel as if you live in a museum,"

he said. "The kitchen has to be comfortable, and not a statement about authentic design."

BEFORE YOU START

SOLID FRAMEWORK If you're buying a house, look for one with a good floor plan and solid basic "bones." A house with a solid framework that won't require compete gutting is probably best—for your peace of mind and your budget.

REFERRALS Get as many bids for remodel work as possible—and follow up on all referrals. Ask contractors lots of questions.

REMODELED It's usually best to buy a house that hasn't been extensively remodeled already. Otherwise, you pay for the remodel, which is often not of good quality or not in the style or materials you want. It may also be dated.

INSPECT Call in a structural engineer, a building inspector, and possibly an architect before you buy a house with a view to remodeling. They can find concealed dry rot, inspect the construction, and look into electrical and mechanical systems.

CONSULT Consult with an architect to find creative solutions for dark rooms or

rabbit-warren floor plans from which you want to carve out a handsome new kitchen. An architect can also estimate costs of renovation—which are always higher than most homeowners expect.

SCALE Don't go overboard. The finished remodel should be appropriate in scale and style to the house and the real estate values of the block.

DECISIONS Know going into the work that there will be an overwhelming series of tiny decisions—from the style of drawer pulls to paint color, faucets, window hinges, wainscot, countertops, tiles, and trim. If you want to be closely involved, set aside time to research materials, hardware, paints, and finishes.

RENOVATION A renovation will probably take more time and money than you anticipate. Be sure to set aside approximately 15% over the bid amount as contingency for unexpected or concealed conditions of the house. Plumbing or wiring may need to be replaced.

LEFT Kitchen designed by Julie Atwood, Santa Rosa.

OPPOSITE Close-up view of Terrence O'Flaherty's shipshape kitchen (see page 35).

SELECTING A DESIGNER

San Francisco kitchen designers Steven and Joan Livingston have planned hundreds of kitchens. Here they help you get beyond "packaged" kitchen design.

Choosing the best designer for your kitchen project is crucial to the success of the designer — and your happiness.

One of the best ways to find the professional that's right is to ask friends whose new kitchens you admire. Did they have a good experience? Would they recommend their designer or architect?

Good designers are attuned to the nuances of working with clients and encouraging individuality. They also love an enthusiastic client, one who stays involved and imaginative throughout the project.

In selecting the perfect professional to design your new or to-be-remodeled kitchen, keep these thoughts in mind:

Find a Specialist. Work with a designer or architect who specializes in kitchens. Seek out someone who has had many years of experience in kitchen design and renovation and who understands every aspect of kitchen design. You will get the best value for your money — and the fewest headaches and surprises — if you work with a professional who has an in-depth knowledge of appropriate materials, equipment, lighting, and floor plans. Even if you're working with an interior designer or architect on the whole house, a kitchen specialist can complement the overall design and give you something special. You want a professional with style, an expert with vision, and an ally with the resources, focus, and hard work to get it all done.

Check References. Even if you've had a great meeting with your kitchen designer and feel you have a won-

derful rapport (or are soul mates), you may be asking for trouble if you don't check all references. The kitchen is a great investment of money and time. You must check that your designer has satisfied previous clients and that he or she has a solid career of completing projects on time. This is the time to find out if the designer is punctual for meetings, has a well-run office, is reliable, and has good follow-up.

Choose a Versatile Architect/Designer. Some designers can complete one style — perhaps Arts & Crafts or French Country — very well. Their ten-year kitchen-design career may be solid but they may only do traditional styles well. Contemporary or eclectic styles may be outside their range. Look for completed work in their portfolio that reflects or suggests a design direction and vision similar to yours.

Be Articulate. All designers dream of clients with a sure sense of personal style and a strong point of view. They appreciate good direction from clients since the vision can be the basis of a successful project. Don't

ABOVE A cheerful San Francisco kitchen designed by architect Christopher Bigelow. Custom-designed floor by Bigelow.

OPPOSITE Los Angeles restaurant/food guru Merrill Shindler's kitchen is hyper-efficient. Designer: Michael Berman.

imagine that designers want carte blanche to do whatever they wish. They want to please you. A successful outcome for a conscientious designer is a kitchen that makes you happy—and fulfills your requirements.

It's Your Kitchen, Not the Designer's. Some homeowners are intimidated by the designer's or architect's opinions and "strong suggestions." It's best not to be wishy-washy. If you've done your homework and are very clear and confident about what's perfect for you, stick to your guns.

Keep the Peace. Don't work against the designer but with him or her. Don't knock down every idea, recommendation, and pointer that the architect offers. Don't feel that you have to "win" every discussion and "beat out" the designer over each and every decision.

Maintain harmony—in your relationship and in the design. Value and listen to the designer's ideas and solutions. Be respectful—you'll learn more.

Go Beyond a "Packaged" Design. An experienced designer should also be an adventurous and imaginative designer. Formulas for floor plans, countertop sizes, placement, and cabinet styles are meant to be guidelines only. Specific requirements, actual space, and custom design are another matter. A versatile professional should be able to interpret your needs, your style, your comfort, your floor plan, and make it sing.

OPPOSITE French cafe-style chairs, granite counters, and a large skylight make this kitchen comfortable and practical.

BELOW Arts & Crafts lamps, a custom island add shine and personality to this kitchen designed by Julie Atwood.

MICHAEL D. CHIARELLO

Tra Vigne restaurant has been one of the most admired restaurants in the Napa Valley since it opened in 1987. Michael Chiarello was born and raised in the California Central Valley town of Turlock. His family was originally from Calabria. Chiarello is the author of *Flavored Vinegars* and *Flavored Oils*. He recently opened Tomatina, a casual pizza and pasta restaurant adjacent to Tra Vigne, and Caffe Museo in the new San Francisco Museum of Modern Art.

Michael Chiarello lives in the heart of the California wine country and has strong opinions about kitchens, working efficiently in a kitchen, and the sheer pleasure of a practical, beautiful kitchen.

Winter or summer, you can find him cooking in the kitchen at Tra Vigne. Few pleasures of the Napa Valley are sweeter than summer dining in Tra Vigne's garden. As golden light diffuses the western hills, the scent of salad greens, jasmine, the best Napa Valley vintages, and platters of grilled meats fills the air.

Michael and his wife, Inez, are building a new house and a new kitchen. They have given considerable time and thought to what the ideal kitchen would be. Many of the best aspects of professional kitchens, they've decided, are indispensable at home, too.

"I'm not a clutter freak," said Chiarello. "I need to see everything I need and have a clean counter at the same time. I really like clean, open spaces. I think you work best when everything in the kitchen is in order, and equipment and ingredients are in logical, appropriate, convenient places. Every surface and material must be washable."

DIFFERENT STYLES

When you're cooking, the idea is to be comfortable — and that means everyone who cooks in the kitchen must be considered. Inez and I are both chefs, but we have different styles. She cleans up as she goes along. I'm a clean-up-when-I'm-finished kind of guy. One may be completing a dessert, and the other a savory at the same time. We need well-lit separate spaces. Some people can cook in a small space; many can't. Plan so that you don't cramp each other's style.

COUNTERS
I'm moving away from wood. I like the durability and easy-to-clean practicality of marble and granite for working counters, for baking and heavy-duty work.

RHEOSTAT ON THE VENTILATION SYSTEM
When I'm entertaining, I want to be able to crank up the power. For everyday usage, the regular household level is satisfactory, but if you entertain a lot, you may wish to investigate more sophisticated controls.

DISPLAY THE BOUNTY
Big bowls of fruit, such as lemons, pomegranates, or persimmons in season, remind you of the earth's bounty.

REFRIGERATOR
Now that I've spent the past few years testing recipes for my cookbooks at home, I know I must have a step-in refrigerator with a semi-cold area in the entrance. Not everyone needs this, but some large households or people who entertain seriously and a lot should investigate a more sophisticated refrigerator.

STORAGE
There are many aspects of cooking that people don't consider when planning storage. Food and cooking ingredients should be stored at the appropriate temperature. For example, everyone wants to put olive oil next to the stove, but a hot place is not ideal for fine olive oil. I like the idea of a small, insulated, cool, roll-top cubby in the kitchen. Keep the olive oil and your collection of spices and flavorings there. And so that you don't have to make last-minute pre-dinner trips to your wine cellar, keep a daily mini-cellar in the kitchen. Store a few of your favorite wines there—

or a case or two that you can dip into. Be sure that everyday ingredients are close at hand—and stash exotic spices or seasonal ingredients that you seldom use in their own section at the back of the pantry.

APPLIANCES Cooking is really very hands-on. More than 75 percent of your work is done on a cutting board. Therefore, I think that appliances, other than perhaps a toaster or coffee maker, don't have to be kept all over the counter. Store them out of your way—and avoid clutter. Position your work area carefully and make sure that the cutting board is the right height, easily accessible with knives at hand.

INDUCTION COOKTOP I would spend $3,000 in my home kitchen for a single induction burner. I've heard that the prices of these cooktops will be coming down, but whether they do or not, if I have just 16 minutes to cook a meal, with this burner I can accomplish it. It's ten times faster than a normal burner, and it keeps the kitchen cool.

OVEN If I'm cooking for twenty or forty people, I want to put in two turkeys. I need an oven large enough to accommodate them, even if it's just a few times a year. I also like the idea of having a convection feature in the oven—that can be turned on and off as needed.

KITCHEN TABLE I strongly recommend a big, huge dining table. It feels generous and welcoming. A great table of beautiful wood is as important as great food.

ABOVE Chef Ken Hom keeps everything in its place.

OPPOSITE Tiles used artfully by designer Julie Atwood.

IDEAS FROM AN OPINIONATED ARCHITECT

Your budget may not stretch all the way to your dream kitchen. But with help from Toby Levy you will get a smart, satisfying kitchen design.

San Francisco architect Toby Levy has been designing houses and kitchens for more than fifteen years. She recently completed a new house and contemporary kitchen for herself and her extended family.

Toby believes that it is best to create a simple, flexible plan. And to avoid trendiness or trickiness in the design. "Kitchens, new or remodeled, work best when they are straightforward and well integrated with the whole house," she said. "The materials and color scheme must be harmonious and consistent with adjacent rooms. The kitchen must not look as if it landed directly from Mars or belongs in another house."

Toby Levy warns that doorways should be well positioned and that sight lines from the kitchen to the dining room should be carefully considered so that privacy and intimacy are achieved. The architect worked recently with a client who was chemically sensitive and recommends choosing nontoxic, easily maintainable cabinets, countertops, cupboard interiors, paints, and other finishes.

Here are more of her recommendations for a fine, aesthetic outcome to your new kitchen plans:

Pantries. See if you can squeeze a pantry into your floor plan. Walk-in pantries are a very efficient, neat, and accessible way to plan storage. With a pantry close by, you always know where the flour, sugar, raisins, turmeric, gelatin, baby food, soup mix, and dried pasta are when you need them. A pantry also allows for seasonal storage. For example, you can organize those spices, dried fruits, candied flowers, decorations, and special ingredients you use only around Thanksgiving, Hanukkah, or Christmas time.

Ingredients for winter foods can be set aside, ready to bring forth when you need beans and lentils for hearty soups or dried porcini mushrooms for long-simmering stews.

Storage. Design above-counter storage so that it's easily reachable. Many upper cabinets are too high for everyday access. Long-term storage of buffet platters, trays, champagne flutes, holiday silver, party decor, salad bowls, turkey platters, or pedestal bowls is better accommodated in adjacent cabinets.

Appliances. Select appliances appropriate for the way you like to cook and for your convenience. Locate them nearby. Keep everyday electronic appliances such as toasters and coffeemakers on the countertop (possibly in a rolltop or hideaway appliance "garage") so that they're at hand every morning. Be careful of large commercial ranges. They may look great, but are they self-cleaning? Unless you have help, you may not want to tackle cleaning these giants yourself.

ABOVE San Francisco interior designer Orlando Diaz-Azcuy selected Metro metal shelves for practical, handsome kitchen storage.

OPPOSITE This kitchen is custom-fit for its owners. Note the granite counters, and the table for quick snacks. Kitchen designed by Lou Ann Bauer, San Francisco.

Cabinets. Custom cabinetry is fine furniture built into your kitchen. Make it special by selecting finishes, woods, and materials that are striking and complete them in an individual manner. Otherwise, you may be better off with manufactured cabinets and inserts that can be purchased for customization.

Keep It Simple. Being relentlessly modern or overly complicated in kitchen design is not always a good idea. Some colors, materials, or approaches date fast.

An elaborate, highly patterned kitchen can seem restless, busy, lacking in soul. Rather, look at the seventeenth and eighteenth centuries for inspiration. Old, classic materials have validity and purpose. Stones, wood, fine craftsmanship, and simply articulated windows have great presence and visual power.

Look at the charming simplicity and resonance of long-ago rooms with natural ventilation, spacious pantries and larders, simple hardworking counters and very functional tools. Think of the pleasure of a farmhouse kitchen with simple cabinets, sunshine pouring in the windows, waxed wooden floors, a welcoming old table with comfortable chairs. Overly designed kitchens, in comparison, look pretentious and don't, after all, guarantee more delicious food or a happier dining experience.

OPPOSITE A country kitchen with soul, this Napa Valley room combines rough stone and sleek materials. Architects: Byron Kuth and Elizabeth Ranieri, San Francisco.

BELOW Crisp, simple, modern styling is the key to this Southern California kitchen. Note the symmetry of windows and sinks—for harmony. Architect: Michael Sant.

LEARN FROM THE EXPERT

**Follow kitchen designer Julie Atwood as she shares her design wisdom.
She knows the pitfalls and how to avoid them.**

Sonoma County interior designer Julie Atwood is an accomplished kitchen designer. She is also the owner of Art for Living, a design and regional crafts store in Petaluma. Atwood lives in a renovated ranch house in a picturesque valley near Glen Ellen. "Kitchens give you so many opportunities for creativity," she said. "You start and end your day there. A great kitchen makes you feel good."

Julie Atwood's advice is helpful whether you're planning a new kitchen, or starting a remodel. "No architect or designer can give you one simple formula to follow," she said. "Every kitchen needs different ingredients." Experiment and be creative to get your own best recipe.

Cabinets

↜ Planning carefully will ensure that everything has a place—and is accessible when you need it. First ask yourself what you want from your cabinets. What functions must they perform? Is style a priority, or is simple storage the main concern? Are they for display or must everything be put away?

↜ Inventory what you need to store or show. One way to do this is to open your cabinets and take Polaroids. Or you might make lists of all your pots and pans, china, glassware, spices, gadgets. List everything from wraps to sugar, griddles, utensils, bottles of oil, mugs, and cereal boxes. Lists and graphic images begin to give a realistic picture of how much stuff you have and how it might best be contained.

↜ Make separate lists of things that should be at hand daily, and things like roasters, party platters, trays, and festive glasses that can be stored in less accessible places. Everyday water glasses, salad bowls, spices, and coffee cups must be placed conveniently.

↜ Edit everything now. Donate old mugs, plates, jars, pans, and outmoded equipment or duplicates to charity.

↜ Add new equipment currently on your wish list — a bread machine, a new juicer, pasta makers, or champagne flutes — to your storage list. Plan spaces for them.

↜ No one cabinet dimension or system works for everyone. For some families, plates and mugs should be stored in lower roll-out drawers. For others, copper stock pots and paella pans take pride of place. To get a good idea of how much space cooking utensils might need, arrange pots and pans on the counter or on the floor in the way you'd like to store them. Measure the total dimensions. Do the same with plates and cups, glasses, and bowls. Make sure you have room for your biggest bowls and equipment.

ABOVE San Francisco designer Candra Scott added metal mesh with easy-access shelves to her retro cabinets.

OPPOSITE In kitchen designer Julie Atwood's ranch kitchen, timbers, metals, and stone counters are all industrial-strength.

↣ Don't make cabinets too deep. Extra-deep lower cabinets may make upper cabinets inaccessible. Too-deep upper cabinets may make items in the back hard to reach.

↣ Consider the context of your house, and its age. Simple cabinetry is usually best. Avoid overstyled, glitzy cabinetry—inside or out.

↣ To save on cabinetry costs, consider an artful custom-painted finish for standard unfinished cabinets.

↣ Instead of filling your kitchen with cabinets, be inventive with Japanese chests, old pie safes, a breakfront, or an inherited chest of drawers for storage.

↣ For a large, boisterous family, select the hardest finish for cabinets. Compare manufactured and custom cabinet finishes with off-the-rack cabinets for cost and durability.

Sinks

↣ In general, the bigger the sink, the better you'll like it. Deeper, wider, larger sinks are simply more functional. If you'll have only one sink, make it large.

↣ Double bowls are useful if you must have a cleanup and preparation sink. They're also useful in a small kitchen. Many cooks, however, find one large sink more versatile.

↣ Stainless steel is easiest to clean and blends well with other kitchen materials. It won't chip or rust. Enameled cast-iron sinks are quieter and very easy to clean. Designers and chefs like copper, which

---

DOING IT YOURSELF

STYLE The best kitchen design is personal. First fantasize. Don't follow a set theme or a cookie-cutter look. What do you love? Trust your instincts. Believe in your own style.

EXAMINE Take a closer look at what works now. If it's not broken, don't fix it. Changing everything may not be necessary.

CONSULT Study code requirements. Consult local code manuals and safety information at local builders' book resources.

TROUBLESHOOT Consider hiring a troubleshooter before you start construction. When you've refined plans, hire an architect or designer for a flat fee to critique it. Your plan can only get better, more refined—and be validated.

BUDGET If your budget is limited, establish priorities. You may not need to improve ventilation, put in a new floor, and get new cabinets all in one fell swoop. Work out a plan.

INFORMATION If you can't hire an architect, avail yourself of every bit of free information. Visit a home show, poke around the local hardware store and library, or take a design workshop at a local college or builders' supply company. Read every design book and magazine—even take cooking classes.

ABOVE Everything in its place: a spice drawer keeps everything at hand next to the stove.

OPPOSITE Beautifully calibrated woodwork in a Berkeley kitchen designed by Fu-Tung Cheng.

usually must be custom-made. It's warm and friendly and gives instant cachet.

↬ Consider putting a preparation sink near the stove (with space in between for pots and pans). Or place it at the end of a counter for use as a wet bar.

↬ If you entertain a lot, add a small sink beneath the glass cabinet for rinsing glasses and champagne flutes.

Faucets

↬ Decide whether style or function is the most important factor. Do you want old-fashioned style or modern convenience?

↬ A single mixer faucet may be more convenient than hot/cold faucets. A single mixer saves space.

↬ Choose what you love. A traditional kitchen can have modern faucets—or you can use highly detailed antique faucets. Mixing styles is not inappropriate. You may get more pleasure from a whizzy modern

Scandinavian style. You can also rummage in a demolition yard for Victorian faucets or for old French faucets that remind you of a Parisian hotel.

↬ Don't scrimp by buying poor-quality fixtures or unsuitable designs. Buy the best. You use them countless times each day.

↬ Take your local water supply into consideration. Hard water may corrode or clog certain faucets. Check with your local plumbing supply company or plumber. Talk to a plumber before buying.

Lighting

↬ Don't limit your lighting to overhead lighting or task lighting. No one light does it all. A designer can give you practical light—and a wide variety of practical and mood lighting. Consider mixing modern and antique. And don't forget romantic candlelight.

↬ Don't knock fluorescent lighting. There are now dimmable and full-spectrum varieties. A combination of fluorescent and incandescent may work well. Also consider halogen for spots and extra sparkle.

↬ Consider antique or salvaged light fixtures for character. Be sure to have them restored and rewired by professionals.

↬ Plan for atmosphere. Consider a chandelier, torchères, sconces, vintage lamps.

↬ Hire a licensed electrical contractor to install new lighting or vintage lights, or to rewire your kitchen.

ABOVE Custom lighting adds Arts & Crafts character. Kitchen design by Nancy Lind Cooper.

OPPOSITE In Julie Atwood's Glen Ellen kitchen, counters offer acres of work space. Note: easy-access storage.

Sausalito and Napa Valley-based restaurant designer/restaurateur Pat Kuleto has designed some of the most enjoyed and influential restaurants of the last fifteen years. He designed Fog City Diner in San Francisco and has created restaurants from Los Angeles to Tokyo, from Atlanta to Texas — and is in demand to create more.

In downtown San Francisco, Kuleto draws diners to his Kuleto's restaurant for its friendly atmosphere and whole-hearted Italian flavors. Kuleto also designed Wolfgang Puck's Postrio, and McCormick & Kuleto's at Ghirardelli Square. Boulevard on the Embarcadero, where chef Nancy Oakes wields her knives and pans, is another Kuleto masterpiece. And Kuleto has just completed and opened a new restaurant on Post Street, near Union Square.

As he does when creating a restaurant, Kuleto recommends looking for architectural objects at salvage yards when you're planning a new kitchen or beginning a remodel. The beauty is that you don't know what you'll find. It's serendipity. Kuleto incorporated one-of-a-kind treasures into the design of Boulevard, and has worked old metal columns, a handsome bar, wagon-wheel rims for a light fixture, architectural timbers, banisters, and a fireplace mantel into other restaurants. Restored or left as-is, old flooring, antique tiles, copper sinks, brackets, faucets, shelves, and old cupboards can add character and depth to a kitchen restoration or a new kitchen. Many of these old window frames, stained-glass panels, tiles, and timbers cannot be found today, so you'll be involved in the creative recycling of beautiful artifacts.

Kuleto likes to showcase food, art, and architectural details. At Postrio, Kuleto designed a central tile-topped counter lit by low-voltage lights for showcasing pastries and cakes. He suggests setting up vignettes of fruit, wine, flowers, liqueurs, fresh vegetables, or favorite china and lighting them with a well-placed low-voltage light. "Don't just have a glare-bomb overhead light in your kitchen," Kuleto said. "It's harsh and flat and hard on the eyes." Easy-to-install, low-voltage lighting gives a jewel-like color, sparkle, and liveliness to a kitchen. It's also useful lighting for work surfaces.

FLOORPLAN TIPS FROM PAT KULETO

Bay Area designer/restaurateur Pat Kuleto serves up floorplan tips to take home:

FLOW In restaurant kitchens, one of the most important parts of planning is getting the "food flow" right. No one thinks of this at home! As you work out the design of your kitchen, picture the food coming in from the grocery. Unloading and putting away groceries should be fast and easy. Dry storage and the refrigerator should be close by. A large pantry with carefully designated places for everything from cereal boxes to jams and drinks makes unpacking swift.

PREPARATION When you start food preparation, your prep area and produce-washing sink should be close to the refrigerator. You should not have to carry lettuces and fruit, milk, eggs, and carrots across the kitchen.

PROXIMITY The garbage disposal or an organic-material container should be near the counter where vegetables are cleaned and prepared.

ADJACENT The work counter should be adjacent to the sink for quick washing and rinsing. That counter should be within a few steps of the stove. Store or hang pots and pans near the stove.

EASE To ensure ease of cleanup after plates are brought from the table back to the kitchen, then cleaned and dried, be sure that the cabinet for storing plates is not far from the dishwasher or sink.

STATIONS Set up work stations in the kitchen where everything appropriate is at hand. You don't want to be tango-ing all over the kitchen, back and forth, getting a knife or fetching the flour and trying to find a whisk or a certain pan.

FIREPLACE If you're starting on a renovation, investigate a pizza oven, a wood-burning brick oven, or a fireplace. Not only can you broaden your range of home cooking, but a fireplace adds great life and comfort to a kitchen — and flavor to your food.

OPPOSITE Sharon Gillin's Northern California kitchen: ceiling-height cabinets maximize storage.

BELOW In Alice Erb's Oakland kitchen: folk art.

STYLING A KITCHEN

Imaginative styling can refresh an old kitchen without the cost of a major remodel. Don't forget seasonal flowers and generous baskets of vegetables.

San Francisco photo stylist Karen Nicks is in great demand to infuse warmth and style into catalogue photographs of furniture and room vignettes for clients like Pottery Barn. Her confident eye and hand bring together simple, unpretentious objects that suggest signs of life and days of quiet enjoyment.

Nicks believes that experiments with unusual containers, vintage prints, and food-related graphics bring vitality and humor to a kitchen.

"Great styling is food for the eyes," she said. Following are some of Nicks's ideas for styling.

↦ Italian, Greek, or French food cans with colorful labels are inexpensive vessels for bouquets of garden roses, nasturtiums, or ranunculus. These authentic cans can always be found in specialty stores, such as the Italian groceries in San Francisco's North Beach and in New York's Chinatown. Plus, you get to eat the tomatoes, lychees, peppers, and olives!

↦ Antique plates in a variety of sizes, shapes, and tones of white can be grouped together on a wall. It's a fine way to add texture without color to an all-white kitchen. Select lacy creamware, old English ironstone, restaurantware, and gold-rimmed antique white plates. Stand them on shelves or balance them on hooks.

↦ A miniature lemon tree, a topiary of scented geranium, a blooming lavender bush, parsley, chives, varieties of basil, nasturtiums, or marjoram growing in aged terra-cotta pots will cheer you up on the gloomiest day. The scent is very refreshing and you can use the flowers or herbs in a salad. Fresh flowers always look pretty on a newly iced cake.

↦ Gather up photographs of family and friends enjoying themselves at parties and celebrations over the years. Include everyone: school friends, church picnics, toddlers' first steps, your two-year-old eating birthday cake, your in-laws toasting their fiftieth wedding anniversary, the whole gang on the back lawn eating watermelon. Have black-and-white prints made of your originals. Have them mounted and framed in simple museum frames like precious art. Hang in a grouping on the wall and add more over time. Voila! The story of your life.

↦ One flea-market print or two is nice, but often more is better. There's strength in numbers. Good vintage kitchen prints include bird eggs, pears, leaves, or fancy French desserts. Start a collection. Pressed garden flowers on long stems can look very elegant in simple wooden frames.

ABOVE In Sharon Gillin's kitchen: heirloom tomatoes in a bowl, tomato plants, and a tomato red tabletop.

OPPOSITE Nick Mein improvised his charming kitchen from an old stable tack room. Herb topiaries, orchids, prints, antiques, and rugs all delight the spirit.

⌁ Old school clocks and service station clocks from rural America look very graphic grouped on the wall. Instant nostalgia! They don't have to be in working order.

⌁ Consider vintage utensils and molds as wall sculpture. The odd shapes of old metal candy molds, metal scoops, jelly molds, cookie cutters, tongs, or old ladles and graters give you a sense of the past — and make you grateful for some modern conveniences.

⌁ If you don't have much room in your kitchen, hang decorative wall brackets and stand Chinese exportware, Arts & Crafts vases and pitchers, even large shells on them.

⌁ Flowers are great in a kitchen — especially if they are picked from your own garden. Rather than arranging, which usually looks too formal, put a simple but generous armful of the same flowers in a glass cylinder vase, or in a wide-mouthed urn. Imagine three or four bunches of pink tulips, or a couple of bunches of white or yellow daisies in a big white pitcher or an old glass vase. With glass, you can see the stems and that's part of the pleasure. Simple inexpensive daffodils, garden roses, lilac, and rubrum lilies are very cheerful.

⌁ Large, thick cylindrical glass vases filled with lemons, limes, pomegranates or green apples are more interesting than the usual bowl of fruit. (The Calvin Klein Home collection has some rather austere but handsome cylindrical vases.)

TIP

Above all, if you're going to go to the toil and trouble and expense of remodeling, make sure that the finished design has your signature. That may be a marble-topped counter for pastry making, a grill, witty drawer pulls, handcrafted tiles, retro-rich colors, the luxury of spacious closets, acres of storage, handsome Craftsman-style cabinets, rooms for an armchair, a built-in office, or a library for your cookbooks.

ABOVE Metal shelves are practical, sturdy, and versatile.

RIGHT Granite and tile make a handsome combination. Faucets here are true hard-workers.

OPPOSITE White is the perfect background for this very charming, off-kilter kitchen.

NANCY OAKES

Nancy Oakes is the very popular chef/owner of Boulevard, the bustling restaurant in the historic Audiffred building on the waterfront in San Francisco. Nancy and her husband, sausage-maker/author Bruce Aidells, live in Kensington, east of San Francisco. They remodeled their turn-of-the-century house (and kitchen) last year.

LIGHTING Plan well-modulated overall lighting, as well as focused task lighting. Create pleasing, not harsh, ambient lighting. Be careful not to create shadows. Working at a poorly lit counter or without sufficient light over the stove can lead to kitchen injuries.

WORK SURFACES Think about what you really do day-to-day in your kitchen, along with what you cook

and how you prepare it. For our house, we wanted work surfaces that are easy to maintain. We avoided granite and moved toward wood for its warmth and natural antiseptic qualities. For hardworking, much-used areas, we chose stainless steel for efficiency and easy maintenance.

FLOORS We installed maple floors and sealed them with polyurethane — the most rugged variety.

SINKS For many people, sinks are an afterthought. But you should consider how you cook and the kind of equipment and tableware you use. Do you need a sink that holds large pots and pans and cookie trays? Will your pasta pot fit under the nozzle? We installed a commercial stainless-steel dishwashing sink without dividers. The dividers have very limited actual use. With a big, serviceable sink, you'll have a lot less water on your kitchen floor.

AESTHETICS If you don't cook much, your kitchen can be very design oriented. If you really like cooking, and cook a wide variety of

dishes and foods, you need to make your kitchen work for you. Be realistic as well as aesthetic. If you bake or can a lot, you need a specialized setup, with appropriate surfaces and every ingredient at hand. You need generous counter space. When you're planning a kitchen, don't forget to make room for guests. Make them part of the picture, but keep them out of the traffic line between the stove and the work surface. Design a space where they can sit or stand comfortably (with a wine glass in hand) while you complete the cooking.

OVENS Two ovens are a must for a family cook who loves to cook for company. It's impossible to prepare a celebratory or holiday meal without them. If possible, at least one of them should have a convection feature for better browning.

DINING ROOMS Do you want a separate dining room? What is your style of entertaining? We made our kitchen and dining into one large informal room. This works with our lifestyle and our way of entertaining, which is welcoming and casual.

GARBAGE Make sure your garbage is easily accessible — especially if you plan to use it for compost. Our garbage container is discreetly but conveniently placed at the end of the kitchen counter.

SLIDE RACKS Hot food comes out of the oven — especially during the holidays when you have roasts, cookies, bread — and this is the time when you will love or hate your kitchen. Every recipe tells you to set aside everything that comes steaming and bubbling and spattering out of the oven. Where will you set it aside as you go on with the preparation of other dishes? You may have ample counter space, but I have another solution. In restaurants, we have steel rolling speed racks to hold large, flat trays from the oven. Install one of these (available from restaurant supply stores) under your upper cabinet and up off the counter, and be sure it has ventilation.

COUNTER SURFACES It's not always the size, but where work surfaces are located that's important. Don't put primary working

counters beneath wide, overhead cupboards. You need room to work in — without worrying about banging your head. Ideally kitchens should have a work surface opposite the stove. Then everything is at hand — and you can keep an eye on the progress of what-

ever's cooking on top of the stove or in the oven. There's something to those old-fashioned ideas about work triangles. You should not be running hither and thither all over the kitchen. You prepare food on the counter, you cook, you serve, then you wash up.

Make your kitchen layout logical and convenient for these tasks.

Above all, enjoy your cooking — whether you have your dream kitchen or you're still planning it. Buy the best seasonal ingredients, experiment occasionally, and make every

meal memorable — whether it's for yourself or company.

ABOVE Nancy Oakes and Bruce Aidells's kitchen is clearly a room for food professionals — and people who simply love to cook. There's room for two to cook, and hardworking, practical surfaces.

FINESSING FLOORS

The perfect floor is your foundation for great kitchen design. Practicality, easy maintenance, and beauty must go hand in hand.

San Francisco designer/contractor Lou Ann Bauer has remodeled hundreds of kitchens in a wide range of styles and sizes.

"No one material is perfect in every situation, not even hardwood, so it's important to understand what's appropriate for you," said Bauer. "Planning function is the first consideration, but selection is the most satisfying and fun."

Avoid designs, colors, and finishes that are very of-the-moment and will date your kitchen with the year they were done. Timeless, classic design is often best, said Bauer, especially when it comes to floors.

Concrete

You can select 3/4-inch-thick tiles or poured-in-place concrete that's generally 2 inches thick. Concrete can be colored, patterned, and textured in any color and mixed in a variety of finishes. It's very durable and resistant to wear and can be coordinated with countertops. Some homeowners find concrete hard on their feet and legs if they stand for a long period. This is relatively inexpensive flooring but labor and installation charges can add on. And anything that falls on the floor will surely break.

Wood

Oak, maple, and cherry hardwoods are popular. They come in various widths and thicknesses, as well as stained from light to dark. Pine and fir softwood floors can be stained light or dark, but are less durable. Woods give a room a warm glow and are comfortable to stand on for long periods. Consider patterns such as parquet, or stencilled borders or patterns created by a paint finish artist. Dropped plates won't break on wood floors. Wood with the right finish is easy to maintain with light washing. Families with pets or young children may find that wood floors get water damage and scratches. Regular maintenance is required, and refinishing may be required after heavy wear.

Vinyl

Sheet vinyl comes in many widths and a multitude of qualities, colors, and patterns. Styles range from contemporary to traditional. Vinyl tiles, generally 12 inches by 12 inches, come in solid colors and patterns, and both residential and commercial grades are available. Tiles can create many patterns and effects. Vinyls are usually very cost effective and simple to clean. Avoid trendy patterns or faddish colors.

Tile and Stone

Ceramic tile sizes range from 1-inch-by-1-inch mosaics to 18-inch-by-18-inch pavers. Thousands of colors, finishes, glazes, and patterns — and a multitude of edge tiles and other accents — are available. Granite, marble, and limestone are becoming very popular. Tiles offer a greater variety of colors than slab and are less expensive. Hundreds of kinds of terra-cotta pavers, stone pavers, ceramic tiles, and stone accents are manufactured. When correctly finished, they are easy to maintain and will wear well over time.

OPPOSITE In this kitchen designed by Cecilia Campa for Becker/Zeyko Kitchens, stone pavers are a practical choice.

REMODELING POINTERS: SOME INSPIRATIONS

The finest kitchens reflect the tastes, quirks, collections, and passions of their owners. They work toward avoiding that cookie-cutter look.

Arnelle Kase

San Francisco designer Arnelle Kase's Edwardian house has a handsome and very personal kitchen. Spacious, quirky, and full of her spirit, it combines practical stainless-steel surfaces with a romantic old pine central counter and cartoony collections of Czechoslovakian glassware. Its timeless design is full of ideas for other would-be renovators.

"The most important element in creating my own kitchen was making sure I would want to spend time in it," said Kase. "So I made sure that there were plenty of nooks and crannies to house my collections of antique toys, Czech glasses and vases, handcrafted furniture, Italian cookie tins, and other objects that make me smile."

Kase also divided the working part of the kitchen from the dining side and raised the floor slightly to make the dining area level with the patio. With the addition of French doors leading to a paved terrace, the dining space becomes an outdoor garden space when the doors are flung open.

In designing kitchens (including her own), Kase likes mixing counter surfaces. "I have both plastic laminate (which is easy to maintain) and an antique pine island—for warmth and character. I also use this center pine counter as a buffet," she said. "It looks handsome piled with cracked crab or mounded with salad greens and summer vegetables. It also makes a convenient drinks bar, and a practical spot for holiday baking and food preparation."

And a very practical idea: Buy the best fan possible—remote the motor if noise is an issue.

Lou Ann Bauer

Panelli's Arts & Crafts kitchen, opposite, was updated by designer/contractor Lou Ann Bauer. When the owners of this house purchased the property in 1993, it was in a sorry state. Bauer believes that if homeowners are going to the trouble and expense of a

remodel, the new room should reflect their taste. This couple, both jazz enthusiasts, has a collection of art deco furniture. They wanted their kitchen to be updated, not a period piece, and to mirror their admiration for simple, clean aesthetics. Bauer designed the cabinets in figured cherry with a rich stain and a satin finish. The counters are stainless steel at the work end and green-and-black granite on the serving end. Machined stainless-steel knobs, a pendant light fixture designed by Richard Meier for Baldinger, and the forties aluminum chairs enhance the Moderne look. Photographs of jazz greats by Jim Marshall were framed and hung on the walls, which were painted by Art Decor. The banquette is upholstered in Donghia's "Trebizond."

ABOVE Designer Arnelle Kase, an enthusiastic and accomplished cook, loves jolts of color in her own kitchen.

OPPOSITE A framed collection of jazz musician portraits give this remodeled kitchen timeless grace. The banquette is a space-saver. Designer: Lou Ann Bauer.

Bauer helped the Shermans' turn-of-the-century house, opposite, move into the present. "We had three objectives with this kitchen remodel," recalled the designer. "First, we wanted to modernize an outdated kitchen with new cabinets and new appliances correctly positioned. Second, we had to open up the kitchen and let in more daylight—it had been rather gloomy. Our third goal was to make the house compatible with the California Arts & Crafts style of the rest of the house." Large windows were installed above the sink. The wall between the 12-foot-by-16-foot kitchen and the 12-foot-by-10-foot dining area was torn down and replaced with a useful peninsula. The countertops are green granite. Bauer selected custom walnut-stained maple base cabinets and translucent green-stained wall cabinets. The handmade tiles are by Ann Sacks.

The Staley kitchen, above, was an ambitious re-model. "It was surprising to me that one of the largest Victorian houses in this neighborhood had one of the smallest kitchens," said Bauer. "For the young owners and their three sons, this had to be a multi-functional room with lots of space." Bauer took advantage of every inch she could take from adjoining rooms — and made the most of a few disadvantages that came up. A dividing wall was removed, leaving a deep beam spanning the ceiling. A grid of false box beams was designed incorporating the support beam. Two existing brick chimneys were incorporated into the new kitchen. The central island cooktop with its commanding copper hood suggests the ancient practice of positioning a fire in

ABOVE This small kitchen was remodeled by Lou Ann Bauer to give a sense of spaciousness. Cheerful colors and personal collections give the large room lots of zip.

OPPOSITE Granite counters, boldly patterned tiles, and superb planning make this San Francisco kitchen exceptional. Note the Italian beaded glass shades. Designer: Lou Ann Bauer.

the center of the room. Bauer designed the island cabinet to look like furniture, with decorative brackets and spindle "legs" at all four corners. Chairs are by Grange; the cabinets are by Cottonwood Premier Kitchens. The color scheme is red/orange, verdigris, and white with splashes of persimmon and mustard. The countertop is red-and-black granite. The drawer and door pulls, designed by Bauer, are hand-carved, hand-painted tropical fish.

Lorri Kershner

Santa Cruz architectural designer Lorri Kershner, of L. Kershner Design, is an enthusiastic cook. Her own kitchen wisdom and experience are evident in the subtleties of kitchens she renovates. The Los Altos kitchen design shown here was inspired by the Craftsman sensibilities of the house, which was built in the forties. Her plan was to maintain the original California style, but give it the practicality of con-

temporary style and technology. Drawers were incorporated into lower cabinets for storing everything from large pasta pans to Tupperware.

Kershner selected Juperana Fantastico granite for the countertops. Granite is easy to maintain, impervious to stains, and the perfect surface for cooling just-baked cookies. The cabinets are cherry with a cherry stain and a satin Van Dyke glaze. Cabinet pulls are Haefle "Bow." The island is outfitted with large pullouts that look like cabinets but are actually recycling bins. (They are on each side of the basket shelves.) The cabinets were crafted by Tod Detro of Knotty Hole Woodworks.

ABOVE This counter was especially planned for baking with children close by. The extra sink makes for easy cleanup.

OPPOSITE Broad sweeps of counter, an open plan, and a compact island make this a very practical working kitchen.

COLOR IDEAS

**Follow your heart when selecting the most pleasing color for your kitchen.
Explore paint shops, even consider having paint colors custom-mixed.**

San Francisco colorist Jill Pilaroscia melds psychology, physiology, and aesthetics to design color schemes that range from historic-reproduction palettes to simple, elegant contemporary concepts. Since the founding of her firm, Architectural Color, in 1975, she has designed the paint hues for hundreds of residential interiors, restaurants, offices, and historic houses. Pilaroscia is a worldwide color consultant for the Hewlett-Packard Company. (And she has a daughter named Emerald.)

Pilaroscia says that there is no one formula for creating a successful, pleasing color palette for the kitchen. "There are no wrong colors, only wrong color combinations," she said. "Color choices that are based on appropriateness to the architecture and the style of the house, along with personal preferences, will always be more successful over time than color selections based on current trends, themes, or fads."

↬ Nature-based colors inspired by fruits, flowers, leaves, and vegetables are delicious. Look for subtle shades of fig, dusty rose, apricot, muskmelon, grape, pale peach, celery, mushroom, bamboo, palest lettuce green, or aubergine. Bold, stronger colors are often most successful when layered or given an overglaze. If you want the kitchen to be predominantly white, ivory, or beige, consider one of these unexpected colors as an accent for drawer handles, a painting, base door panels, tile borders, or fabrics. Three colors — white, apricot, and pale pine; or celery green, ivory, and black — are more interesting than a two-note color scheme.

↬ For a French Country-influenced kitchen, use ivory white for the ceiling, a medium-value blue (possibly in an "old plaster" finish) for the walls, and semigloss ivory-white for the trim and woodwork. For the counters and splash, consider handmade French tiles or Delft tiles with a blue-and-white glaze. Stain the wood floor in a light golden tone.

↬ Industrial materials like stainless steel and concrete combine well with dramatic paint colors like vermilion, burgundy, indigo, and eggplant. Adding gloss to the paint will further enhance the tech feeling of the kitchen.

↬ Use the power of contrast to give your kitchen colors more character, more bite. Juxtapose the warmth of cherry wood cabinets with rich blue tones on tiles, on the walls, or on drapery fabrics. Taupe and mushroom colors balance the rich red tones of mahogany furniture. Tomato red, used in moderation on a small wall or on drawer pulls, adds life to black appliances and medium-stained wood cabinets.

ABOVE Candra Scott's colorful thirties collection and garden roses.

OPPOSITE In the East Bay kitchen of Richard and Kaye Heafey, designed by Michael Vincent, subtle apricot/peach tones were used on the walls. It's the perfect foil for a series of framed English rural scenes and an elegant beaded lamp.

All-white kitchens are fresh and pleasing but do need definition and framing so that they don't disappear in a haze of white. Mexican terra-cotta pavers, honed cream or white marble in a rather bold pattern, an unusual wood for countertops or cabinets, antique painted armoires, or vintage pie cupboards with patterned metal doors can bring a white kitchen into focus.

Color is often most successful in a kitchen when it is unexpected. Rustic distressed wood cabinets color-washed in gray/green or blue/green get a boost from pale-apricot walls and a violet-tinted palest-blue ceiling. Also consider the snap of apple green with pine-needle green in a pale wood kitchen. Taupe-, sand-, or clotted cream-colored walls can be a soothing background. If they look a little sleepy, introduce a touch of terra-cotta, perhaps creamy white and pale apricot.

OPPOSITE & BELOW Room with a view: This remodeled kitchen in the Napa Valley was originally a galley-style room with one small window. The ceiling was originally 8 feet high, flat, and claustrophobic. The counters were laminate, and the appliances were very outdated. The key new architectural element is the 12-foot vaulted ceiling and the transom window over the sink. The new custom-milled windows open out to provide unobstructed views of the valley. New cabinets have a hand-rubbed crackle finish. Countertops are integral-color concrete. Appliances include a Sub-Zero refrigerator, Thermador double ovens, a Wolf range with a stainless-steel exhaust hood, and a custom-made 16-inch-deep single-compartment sink. Ceramic tiles are by Ann Sacks. The custom-designed island is an antique pine table with a bead-board cabinet installed below. Kitchen design by Rob Wilkinson of Wilkinson & Hartman Architects, San Rafael.

THOMAS KELLER

Thomas Keller, beloved owner and executive chef of the country-chic French Laundry in Yountville in the Napa Valley, has gained a worldwide following since he took over the restaurant in 1994. The French Laundry regularly turns up on national "best restaurants" lists, and Keller was recently named Best Chef/California at the annual James Beard Foundation Awards. Keller is admired not only for his impeccable taste, but also for the subtle humor he brings to his menus. Guests dine on Tongue in Cheek (braised beef cheek, veal tongue, baby leeks, garden greens, and horseradish cream) and "Coffee and Doughnuts" (cinnamon-sugared doughnuts with cappuccino semi-freddo). Keller's house, adjacent to the restaurant, overlooks raised beds of herbs, lettuce, and vegetables.

CHEF KELLER'S MUST-HAVE KITCHEN LIST

Coffee grinder — for grinding coffee, spices, and powders
Single-sided hand cheese grater
Wagner skillet
Lettuce spinner
Vegetable peeler
Wire whisk
Californian or Italian extra-virgin olive oil and high-quality balsamic vinegar
Toaster oven
Stereo with CDs by female vocalist
Citrus juice press
Measuring cups
Espresso machine
Champagne in the refrigerator
Berkeley Farms sweet butter
Fresh herbs — fresh chervil, year round
Bay leaves, fresh from the backyard tree
Whole cinnamon sticks
Vanilla pods
Pepper mills — for black and white peppers
Fresh cream
Chinois strainer
Bottled waters
Local goat cheese
Napa Valley honey, French honey
Poetic refrigerator magnets
Table wine for cooking
Pruning shears, scissors
String
Paintbrush

JEFF INAHARA

Jeff Inahara has made a splash since he arrived at Vertigo, one of the most stylish and lively restaurants in San Francisco. A veteran of Patina in Los Angeles, and Elka in San Francisco, he likes sophisticated yet gutsy cooking. Inahara, whose grandparents came from Japan, grew up in Oregon on his family's farm. He has worked alongside chefs Traci des Jardins and Hubert Keller, but calls chef Joachim Splichal of Patina his greatest inspiration and influence.

MY KITCHEN ESSENTIALS

Rice and a rice cooker
Extra-virgin olive oil (Tuscan)
A Kitchen-Aid mixer (I always seem to end up making scones and soufflés for house guests)
Frozen chicken stock
A Wolf range with a convection oven
My mom's pickled anything — cucumbers, green beans, green tomatoes, okra
Ice cream — homemade
Window boxes of fresh herbs
Clover Club potato chips
Peet's coffee and tea.
  I particularly like Peet's Major Dickason's blend of teas — it's very refreshing.

PAUL BERTOLLI

Executive chef Paul Bertolli is obsessed with ingredients. He makes his own vinegars, hunts wild boar in the wilds of Sonoma County, goes out early to find the best wild mushrooms. Bertolli is admired internationally for the elegant simplicity of his dishes. Bertolli was for ten years the highly influential chef at Chez Panisse. After writing *Chez Panisse Cooking*, he left there to study medieval philosophy at the University of Toronto. He is now drawing diners to the inviting, Italian ambiance of Oliveto restaurant for his earthy, soulful food.

In addition to importing artisan balsamic vinegar barrels from Modena, he manages the *acetaias* (vinegar barrels) of a number of families in Napa and Sonoma counties. Like Alice Waters, he has cultivated warm, close, appreciative relationships with California purveyors and growers. In the cozy Oliveto dining room, Bertolli displays his own olives and olive oils, vinegars, favorite wines, and great baskets and bowls of seasonal vegetables and fruits.

Now he is also turning his attention to his own kitchen. "I have always wanted a kitchen that felt as though it were in a garden," Bertolli said. "I was lucky enough to purchase a property in the Berkeley Hills that has a marvelous garden. I am now in the process of renovating the kitchen." His dreams for his own new kitchen can inspire kitchen renovators to be a little more ambitious and soulful in their approach.

VIEWS My new kitchen will have large, open views of the garden on just about every side.

FIREPLACE I will have a fireplace, which is crucial for my style of cooking—spit-roasting, grilling, burying things in cinders. We plan to live around the kitchen in adjoining spaces that are open to the kitchen for reading, relaxing, dining, sitting with guests. The fireplace will provide a focus (which is, after all, the Latin word for fireplace).

AIRY Light and air go hand in hand with the open views. I can't stand claustrophobic environments.

ESSENTIALS Other essentials of a good kitchen: A strong, thick slab of maple set in place to use as a cutting surface. Five or six heavy-bottomed sauce pots of various sizes, including a 12-quart braising pot, a 6-quart casserole. These can be enameled steel, or French copper with nickel alloy lining, or laminated aluminum and steel. Nothing too precious.

EQUIPMENT Get the equipment you love to use and bring it out every day. I use a food mill a lot for sauces, ragu, and soup. Good knives are the key to efficient, thoughtful food preparation. Good wooden spoons, a few with angled sides to get into the corners of pans, the whisk and the strainer.

LONGEVITY Don't buy flimsy, temporary pots and pans or knives. I favor seasoned, cold-rolled-steel saute pans over any of the non-stick choices, and couldn't live without my old knives, which I've been using for over 20 years. They belong in my hands now.

STAPLES Get great, basic ingredients. In the larder, I always have good extra-virgin olive oil and balsamic vinegar I make myself. Flour or semolina for pasta is always here. With the garden nearby, these simple staples always supply the basis for a meal when we don't want to shop.

HOME-MADE House-made ingredients and flavorings give your cooking spirit and individuality. Make your own chutneys, jams, sauces, syrups, flavored vinegars, stocks, and seasonal vinaigrettes. I keep a wine vinegar barrel going all the time. I can jams and jellies with ripe, seasonal fruit and make sauces with flavorful vegetables.

SAFETY FOR CHILDREN

Most kitchen accidents can be avoided with thoughtful planning.
Hardware stores are excellent resources when kid-proofing.

Families with young children — or households with young visitors — must take special precautions to be sure that their kitchen is safe and friendly for babes learning to crawl, toddlers, and young children. Think ahead — and check your hardware store for special safety equipment that will safeguard prying fingers, unsteady walkers, and inquisitive eyes. Encourage exploration and learning in other realms.

↢ Youngsters are drawn to explore every waking moment. First-time parents are often surprised by their child's capabilities—and appetite for exploration and discovery. A flour bin, pots and pans, cat food, the back of the VCR, scouring powder, ketchup bottles, or paint tins are endlessly fascinating. When children are just starting to crawl and walk, be sure that cabinet and closet doors are kept closed with special locking fasteners. A variety of door locks and closures are available from hardware stores and can later be detached as children pass this "into everything" phase. Similarly, protect and close drawers that are within reach. Duct tape can be used as a temporary measure.

↢ It is especially important that cupboards and cabinets with household cleaners, alcohol, bug sprays, garden chemicals, or pet food be closed and locked securely. Be sure that garbage cans are securely closed and that contents cannot be reached. Better still, make sure that anything that might prove hazardous or toxic to curious children is kept well out of reach.

↢ Tippy chairs or stools, television sets, rolling carts, and small tables that can easily be pulled over by unsteady toddlers are best put away. Secure small appliances, the stereo, and the VCR.

↢ Never leave the handle of a boiling pot or a kettle protruding over the edge of the stove top. It can too easily be knocked or pulled off the stove, spilling its hot contents. When cooking with hot oil, or when there is a danger of grease spattering, be sure that children are not nearby. In addition, use spatter guards for skillets and sauté pans. Follow safety directions for deep fryers diligently.

↢ Sharp corners are not friendly to adults or children. When planning a kitchen, avoid potentially hazardous sharp edges on tables, counters, and islands. Some children's furniture showrooms have special guards for the corners of tables.

↢ Be sure that electrical wiring is taped out of the reach of young children. Computers and other electronic equipment should be stored away from the edges of home office desks and kitchen counters. Junior scientists will want to have a closer look.

↢ "Blind" covers that temporarily protect electrical sockets and outlets are available at hardware and home-supply stores. Outlets seem fascinating and appear rather harmless to youngsters, so children are often tempted to touch them or play with them. Don't take chances.

OPPOSITE Simplicity assures safety. Architect Heidi Richardson's design: handsome timbers, sculptural lighting, walls of windows. Tiles add texture and graphic interest.

✺ Keep all glass bowls, crystal glasses, bottles, and breakables in a high cupboard.

✺ Many stoves have on/off knobs that remove for cleaning. Either remove them when children are about, or purchase knob caps from home-supply or hardware stores. Do the same with outdoor gas grills.

✺ Kilim rugs or mats in kitchens can trip children who are learning to walk. Either secure them with double-sided tape or use special non-slip matting.

✺ And don't neglect other safety considerations. Other baby-proofing equipment includes gates for tops of stairs, window guards, locks for windows on upper floors, door gates, guard rails, even testers to check for lead in the water.

And consider your own safety. Encourage children to keep their skates, balls, toys, books, games, and vehicles in their proper storage places — not all over the kitchen floor where they can trip busy adults.

OPPOSITE In this kitchen designed by Rob Wilkinson, the uncomplicated layout makes for safe cooking and easy food preparation.

BELOW Cecilia Campa's deft hand brings an almost Mondrianesque pattern to this kitchen. Straightforward design is soothing — and very safe.

THE FINER POINTS OF KITCHEN CABINETS

Custom-made or off-the-rack? Top-of-the-line or cheapo salvaged?
Clear glass fronted or descreetly obscured? You must decide.

Architect Henry Siegel of Siegel & Strain Architects in Northern California, has designed many handsome, practical kitchens. He has finessed hundreds of kitchen issues—from helping clients avoid trendy colors to tweaking the proportions of cabinets. His pro tips can help you rethink cabinet design.

↣ Proportion of cabinets is important. They must look balanced, and access should be comfortable. Doors should not be too wide or too narrow. Narrow drawers in lower cabinets are not useful because you can't fit much except small spice jars into them. Too-deep drawers can be difficult to access or keep in order. Wide doors can be unwieldy and can warp.

↣ If you want stile and rail (panel) cabinets, proportion the stile (the outer frame) carefully. Don't make it too wide or too skimpy. And don't attempt to match the stile and rail of a door on a narrow drawer. Flat drawer fronts look best with panel doors.

↣ Alignment is important for an overall feeling of harmony and good design. Try to align upper cabinets and lower cabinets where possible. Center sinks beneath windows and above cabinet doors.

↣ Don't build too many cabinets with glass doors or you may create a storage and neatness dilemma. Everything in the cabinets is visible. (You have nowhere to stash vivid Tupperware, old bowls, and half-empty jars and boxes.) Either limit the number of glass doors to just those that house neat displays—or have the glass doors etched, sandblasted, textured, or ridged.

↣ Put a single drawer over every lower cabinet door. You lose little out of the cabinet and gain many useful and easily accessible drawers.

↣ Limit the number of upper cabinets for a cleaner-looking, better-proportioned kitchen. Consolidate what you normally store in upper cabinets into pantries or narrow floor-to-ceiling cabinets that might line an adjacent hallway.

↣ Always ask for full-extension drawer hardware, so that the drawer can be pulled out fully. Don't be talked out of this. It makes everything in your drawer accessible. Heavy-duty ball-bearing slides will last longest.

↣ Use your ingenuity to find more storage space. Use the insides of cabinet doors for spice racks, lid hangers. Hang a small garbage-bag holder on the inside of the cabinet door, beneath the sink.

↣ If you're tall, it's sometimes nice to increase the space between the lower and upper cabinets by as much as six inches. This will also make the kitchen

ABOVE Simple cabinets work well in this space. The design won't date, and the corner counter is very useful.

OPPOSITE Clear glass cabinet fronts display color collections in this handsome kitchen designed by David Lebovitz.

feel more spacious. When the ceiling is higher than eight feet, don't take upper cabinets all the way up to the ceiling. You won't be able to reach the top easily, and the additional cabinetry is expensive. Instead, leave space between the ceiling and the top of cabinets. Add top molding and subtle lighting.

⚮ Door and drawer pulls are important accents, since they are so visible. There are now hundreds of different styles from practical metal knobs to witty silver or gilded handles in the shape of fish, knives and forks, leaves and flowers. Knobs, pulls and handles don't all have to match. And consider using antique or vintage pulls found at a flea market or salvage yard. On a practical note: Be sure that the pull is not too small and that you can easily grip the handle with wet fingers.

⚮ Think green. Recycle existing cabinet "carcasses" whenever possible. For an instant update, just replace door and drawer fronts or reface your cabinet doors. Consider using salvaged lumber or certified environmentally sound veneers for the cabinets. For good, earth-conscious floors and cabinets, contact companies like Eco-Timber in San Francisco for supplies of beautiful woods milled in sustainable forests.

⚮ Cabinets don't have to be fresh-from-the-box. Old architectural treasures can give a new or remodeled kitchen real character and dimension.

OPPOSITE Cabinets have fifties motifs inset. Chicken wire fronts are inexpensive, witty. Design by Agnes Bourne, San Francisco,

BELOW Note the red detailing on Candra Scott's thirties-style cabinets. Plastic pulls are red, too.

ALICE WATERS

Alice Waters founded Chez Panisse in Berkeley more than twenty-five years ago. Since then her gospel — patronize local growers, buy fresh, seasonal fruits and vegetables and cook them simply — has spread throughout the country. Her most recent cookbook, *Chez Panisse Vegetables*, emphasizes flavor, freshness, and the sensual enjoyment of food. Alice lives with her husband and daughter in a Berkeley bungalow. The large, sunny kitchen, remodeled to her specifications, is the focus of the house. It's a comfortable room with all-day sunlight, lots of comfortable chairs, and a door leading straight out to the garden. In her choices of materials, surfaces, and dinnerware, Alice honors tradition. Her plates and cups are a pleasing and poetic mix of old, mismatching patterns. Her sink is copper. Her floor

is hardwood with a subtle stenciled pattern around the periphery. And always there is the scent of vegetables fresh from the earth — and anticipation of glorious food.

FIREPLACE For me, the number one requirement is a fireplace for cooking. I love cooking in the brick fireplace I added in my kitchen when I renovated and enlarged this space. Cooking in a brick oven brings so much flavor to meats, poultry, and vegetables. When the coals are hot, I often put my Tuscan grill into the fireplace and grill vegetables. The fireplace includes a side-by-side bread oven where I can bake pizzas, focaccia, and other breads.

TABLE A good kitchen must have space for a big, generous table. It should be quite large and expandable so that friends can gather in an informal way. You should not feel cramped. My own table has an Italian stone top, simple wooden legs. I have a mixture of antique wooden chairs. It's more interesting if they don't match. Chairs must be comfortable, perhaps with a cushion, so that friends can sit for hours dining and talking into the night.

SINK I like a big, deep sink. Mine is copper, custom made by a fine Berkeley craftsman. I like materials like copper that get a patina over time and show wear. Copper reflects back at you in a beautiful way.

COUNTERS I don't like hard surfaces like stainless steel for counters. My counter top is African "painted" slate which is dark-gray "painted" with copper and glints of mica. When oil gets spilled on it, it just washes off. The slate also has a nice feeling. It's practical but friendly.

FLOORS I love the look and feeling of hardwood floors, but the maintenance is too great. I don't really like floors that show dirt, unless it's an old, old farmhouse wooden floor with no sealer — but that's not really appropriate in a city house. Otherwise, I'd select a tile floor — such as big, old terra-cotta tiles with no high-gloss sealer. That feels friendly, classic, and comfortable in all seasons.

GARDEN If possible, a kitchen should have easy access to a garden. You can look out the window or the open door and see

tomorrow's lunch! I like to be able to go out and pick fresh herbs and lettuces from my garden just before I start preparation of dinner. In fact, I don't decide exactly what we'll eat until I've seen what's at its peak in the garden. The other advantage of a garden just outside the door is that you can sit out there before dinner, wind down, and enjoy an aperitif. You can smell the flowers, watch the progress of your tomatoes or grapes, and dream of the time when everything is ripe. It's nice to be close to the earth.

LIGHT Good, warm light is important. My kitchen has a bay window overlooking the garden and some old trees so it seems filled with light during the day. It also has windows facing west for afternoon light. Ideally, you should have a practical overhead light, and then lamplight for certain tasks, and then a lower level of light for when you're at table. I chose downspots over the counters and sink before I knew better. They're great for cutting on the butcherblock counter, but not really versatile. To improve matters, I've added a lamp on the counter, wall sconces, and an electrified chandelier.

HUBERT KELLER

Every night, limousines line up outside Fleur de Lys, the beautiful downtown San Francisco restaurant where chef/co-owner Hubert Keller works his magic. The flower-filled interiors were originally designed by Michael Taylor. Trained in classic French cooking, Keller has created his own style based on Mediterranean-influenced traditional French cooking that is at once complex, simple, and very sophisticated. He and his wife, Chantal, live in San Francisco. Keller recently published his third cookbook, *The Cuisine of Hubert Keller*.

Hubert Keller lives with his wife in a quiet neighborhood of San Francisco. They have a large kitchen, designed meticulously by the couple, and they love to entertain.

PLAN FUNCTION It's very important to have a functional kitchen with lots of counter space. My kitchen has room on the counter for thirty-five dinner plates, so it works very well when we have friends or family for special dinners. The counter space is designed so that it's not overwhelming. From day to day, I have an antique duck press displayed in the middle of the counter. In my work, I've learned how important it is to have counter space for preparation, and then for plating the dinner. Often when I am cooking at clients' houses, I have to bring in banquet tables for preparation because the clients don't have enough surfaces.

GARDENS It's ideal to link a kitchen with a garden. My kitchen has French doors to a sunny patio, where we can have breakfast on Sunday morning. It has a fountain, so it's very pleasant, very peaceful. I like to be able to barbecue when entertaining. Barbecued food tastes wonderful, and it's easy to clean up.

AESTHETICS When you have a large countertop, it's best if it has some pattern.

It's more interesting, not so monotonous. My countertop is of Tibetan granite. It's dark gray with stripes and markings of dark red. There's a ribbon of stainless steel around the edge.

EQUIPMENT Get equipment right the first time and it will last for decades. Think carefully what you really need for entertaining, even if you don't do it very often. I have a Traulsen refrigerator and freezer, plus an ice maker. I have a Wolf range with two ovens, a salamander, a grill, and six burners. Not everyone needs that much, but some large families could use that equipment every day. Chefs love brick ovens for flavor and special treats. If you have space, add one for making pizzas and bread or for grilling.

LIGHT & SOUND Overhead lighting, lighting under the cabinets, and lighting in the cabinets are important. More important is to be able to change the lighting to suit the activity. I have all of my lighting programmed so that I can change it at the click of a button. I'm always surprised when people have a beautiful, lavish kitchen and a little old radio standing on the

counter. Get a good music system installed, even if you sometimes listen to the radio. My Bang & Olufsen system with a CD player is installed invisibly, and the speakers are concealed. I love to play rock 'n' roll, but sometimes enjoy classical music.

SPACE FOR LIVING If you have children, be sure to keep space so that they can do homework, work on projects, watch television, or read in an armchair. Then the family can spend more time together while dinner is prepared, or while meal clean-up is happening.

A SENSE OF HISTORY Tie your kitchen and cooking in with the past—the history of cooking. Instead of meaningless accessories, display antique or vintage copper pans, old copper or ironstone molds, antique kitchen equipment. Show the real thing, like my antique duck press. Other friends have old French cooking utensils.

EFFICIENT WASHING-UP Have a deep sink for washing special plates, delicate glasses, champagne flutes. Even if you have a dishwasher, you need to wash many things by hand.

QUICK KITCHEN STYLE

Look beyond kitchen clichés and pre-packaged style when "dressing" your kitchen. Flea markets are great hunting grounds.

For those design-conscious homeowners who do not have the money, time, or desire for a total kitchen remodel, interior designer Ann Jones—also a partner in Sloan & Jones, the Sonoma antiques store—has some novel ideas for quick kitchen style.

↜ Put a small lamp on the counter instead of relying on unflattering overhead lighting.

↜ Use mirrors — perhaps vintage ones with mismatching frames — to add sparkle and light to the space. Even tiny mirrors will work.

↜ If the front door panel of your refrigerator or freezer is removable, you can update the look of it with a new custom-made panel. Consider a dark-green or slate chalkboard — a great place for leaving messages or writing reminders, grocery lists, or recipes. Other options include perforated pie-safe metal (old or faux-old), a panel of zinc (which will age and gain character), a sheet of stainless steel, or a sheet of laminate in bright colors.

↜ Consider using open shelving, which requires more maintenance (and tidiness) but puts plates, mugs, and glasses at hand and adds to the welcoming atmosphere and visual pleasure.

↜ Bring in an old armoire, a pie safe, an old pine dresser, or an antique marble-topped table as storage and counter space. They give the kitchen a remembrance-of-times-past mood and add to its efficiency. Old chairs, possibly mismatched and a bit worn, invite friends and family to linger. With vintage furniture, any new nicks, scratches, and spills caused by young children or pets won't add to parent anxiety and will bestow a sense of life and of time passing.

↜ Hang some fine contemporary photographs or watercolors on the walls. (And banish braids of garlic!)

↜ Put a rug on the floor. Not a mundane mat, but a washable vintage rag rug or sisal. If you can find a well-priced (and a bit worn) Oriental carpet or kilim, bring that into the kitchen. It will require a minimum of care — just a quick shake out the back door or a once-a-week vacuum — and bring warmth and comfort to the kitchen.

↜ Use silver, bamboo, or tin trays on the counter to set out oil and vinegar, salt and pepper, and herbs you use every day for cooking. Trays keep everything organized and at hand, and give a sense of order to the kitchen.

↜ Use fresh fruit, nuts, and vegetables as decoration. Go beyond ordinary apples and boring bananas. If you're lucky enough to have cherry trees or vintage apple trees, clip the fruit plus a few leaves. Show them off in an old wire basket. Arrange fresh tangerines, kumquats, Lady apples, or limes in an antique wooden bowl and stand it on the table or counter. Fill an orange or turquoise Fiesta bowl with fresh walnuts and leave a nutcracker on top. In season, buy four

---

OPPOSITE And the winner is . . . Designer Ann Jones borrows graceful old silver trophies, found at flea markets around the world, to hold utensils, old silver.

or five fresh ginger roots and arrange them on a family–heirloom (or Chinatown) Chinese porcelain platter. Pile tiny pink fingerling potatoes in a big white ironstone bowl. Do what good kitchen stylists do: Stand bright green Napa cabbage or bunches of fresh asparagus on a wooden tray. Make fresh, seasonal ingredients a feast for the eye as well as the palate.

↬ Bring fresh flowers in from the garden — or florist — to welcome you as you make early morning  breakfasts. Natural, loose arrangements work best. Find flea-market decal-decorated porcelain pitchers or pressed-glass vases. Consider an old white ironstone pitcher with spring blossoms, a row of vintage medicine bottles with one or two hyacinths or daffodils each. Fresh-picked jasmine, peonies, and freesias are fragrant and uplifting. Imagine branches of white or purple lilacs in a green Arts & Crafts vase or pitcher. Parrot tulips in red and yellow look festive in a modern Finnish glass vase. But don't stop when summer's past. Arrange small branches of autumn leaves in a Mexican terra-cotta water pitcher, or stand twigs of crab apples or Lady apples (with fruit) in old hand-blown glass vases. Just don't torture your flowers — or believe that they have to be in an "arrangement." Leave ikebana to the experts and arrange to please yourself, following no rules.

↬ Display collections of vintage toys, colorful glass vases, ironstone pitchers, Mexican folk art, or fifties lunch boxes to make the "rented" kitchen instantly yours. Line them up along the top of the refrigerator, on a new shelf (Pottery Barn, Ballard, and Crate & Barrel catalogues sell them ready to install), or along the window sill.

↬ Turn old mismatched spoons, knives, and forks into a bouquet. It's the handle you really want to display because it's often monogrammed or engraved. Half-fill a clear glass cylinder about six or eight inches tall with clear glass marbles. Plant the flatware in the marbles with the handles standing up like flowers.

↬ Roll up extra-large European napkins, tie the cylindrical shapes around the middle with lengths of raffia (from florists) or wide French satin ribbon, pile them — a dozen at a time — on battered but shiny silver trays, and set them in the middle of the dining table. Or array them in an antique trophy.

↬ For the perfect example of a collection holding a collection, stand handfuls of old wooden or lacquer chopsticks or silver knives and forks in mismatched vintage green pottery ginger jars. These inexpensive jars can be found (new) in Chinatown groceries or (old) at flea markets. Collections look wonderful along a buffet.

ABOVE Handpainted cabinets and door in Scott Waterman and Brett Landenberger's kitchen. The floor is seagrass-painted in color blocks.

OPPOSITE Julie Atwood designed this outstanding kitchen in an Edwardian house. Large bowls of flowers and a framed print add character.

CHOOSING A COUNTERTOP

**With so many different options, how do you choose the best material?
We consulted an expert who knows counters and all the pros and cons.**

Cecilia Campa, kitchen designer and principal of Becker Zeyko Kitchens in San Francisco, has been designing kitchens in California, Oregon, New York, and Nevada for more than ten years.

She believes that it is important to research countertop materials, fabricators, and installers before beginning a new kitchen design or remodel. Understand your tolerance level for nicks, scratches, marks, and stains on countertops, she suggests. Some homeowners choose copper, stainless steel, or wood because they believe scrapes and dents are signs of life that add character and warmth. For others, a wine-glass ring or fingerprints are flaws to be avoided. Tarnishing on copper is just what some people love. For others, pure white Corian is the ticket because they know exactly what they're getting, and it will look the same in ten years as it does newly installed.

For countertops, Campa leans toward materials with character, individuality, and practicality.

Granite

PRO: It's a natural speckled material from the earth, so it comes in a wide range of colors, luminosities and depths of pattern. Granites from South America, Europe, and Africa are available. Joints are usually invisible. Granite is easy to clean and maintain. Many edge styles can be crafted. Granite is extremely durable and impervious to heat. With granite installation, sinks can be undermounted.

CON: Granite may be expensive, depending on the quality and rarity of the stone selected. Granite is becoming popular and rather common, and therefore may look dated and passé in the next few years.

Limestone

PRO: Great variety of subtle colors and textures. Interesting variations in hues, tones, and depth. It's a natural material with great beauty. Flamed limestone is gaining interest. Its textured surface is perfect for a "rough-hewn" kitchen where a polished, slick surface is inappropriate. Limestone is a wonderful alternative to granite where a newer look is preferable.

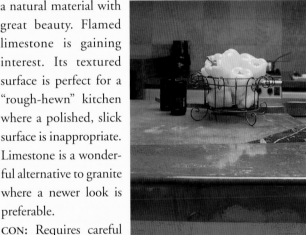

CON: Requires careful maintenance. Certain oils and spices can stain and must be removed immediately. Do not leave spills overnight as the surface is relatively soft. Some homeowners like this somewhat porous quality and love the way curry powder marks, red-wine spills, and olive oil can show signs of life and experience. Clearly, every material is a personal choice.

ABOVE For these counters Fu-Tung Cheng used poured-in-place concrete. It's practical, cost-effective, and can be custom-colored for variety.

OPPOSITE In chef Emily Luchetti's kitchen, contrasting steel and wood add a Mondrianesque geometry to these back-to-back counters.

Soapstone

PRO: An age-old talcum material from South America and Africa that can be buffed to a satiny gloss or used as a matte surface. Custom farmhouse-style sinks can be made with soapstone as well. Often initially appearing a pale gray or taupe, soapstone will oxidize over time and eventually turn almost charcoal or black. Impervious to temperature, acids and chemicals. Very pleasing to the touch.

CON: Not available in a wide range of colors. Limited edging choices. This natural material can vary widely, so choose carefully. It's usually available in 72-inch lengths, so seam placement is a consideration. To maintain soapstone, apply mineral oil every month. This will also darken it.

Copper

PRO: Adds charm, warmth, and an old-world feeling to a kitchen. Not commonly used in residential kitchens, so it adds individuality and character at home. Copper will naturally age and can become marked. Discuss finishes with your installer.

CON: It's expensive. Seams and how to work them in are a consideration. Copper will show signs of use and may become dented or scratched. Copper will tarnish unless treated or finished. It will also show oils from hands and from cooking, and finger marks will be evident. For some homeowners, these signs of life and cooking and family history are a plus.

Concrete

PRO: It's extremely durable and relatively inexpensive. And it now comes in endless colors. One way to give it lots of style, texture, character, and individuality is to add integral tints and dyes as the concrete is mixed. Concrete colors that are particularly hand-some — because they mimic nature — are pale gray and taupe, terra-cotta, pink, muted yellow, and sand. Some experienced concrete-countertop designers and manufacturers can also craft to your specifications, adding fossils, texture, "veins" of color, stones, shells, old coins, plus brass or steel accents into the countertop as it dries.

CON: Can look dark and drab if overused. Joints may be visible. Always work with a skilled fabricator who will mix and pour with no problems and bring design ideas and solutions to your kitchen. Always maintain the concrete according to the fabricator's specifications.

Enameled Lavastone

PRO: Made from lava from France's Massif Central, this material is poured and enameled in any color desired. The surface is glossy and vibrant, slightly crackled. The hard finish is extremely durable, stain resistant, and therefore hygienic. This high-shine surface is a fine alternative to granite.

CON: Costly. Fabricated to order and shipped from France. Long lead time. It's beautiful but needs careful maintenance.

Stainless Steel

PRO: Chefs love it for its sheer practicality and easy maintenance. It's a very versatile material and the gleaming, crisp surface is pleasing to those who savor clean, spotless surfaces. It can look both traditional and timeless, or very contemporary. Sinks can be custom-fabricated and easily integrated with the countertop. It's sterile when cleaned. Surface textures include high polish (for vertical surfaces only), satin,

OPPOSITE Thomas Heinser and Madeleine Corson's city kitchen has straightforward stainless steel counters. Food, newspapers, flowers, and cats keep the low maintenace steel friendly.

quilted, or patterned. Hot pans are not a problem.

CON: Some homeowners think it appears cold. Shine may be undesirable. Steel will show scratches. Marks can be buffed out by a professional with special equipment. It will show fingerprints. Heavy and hard objects dropped on the surface of stainless steel counters will leave dents. For many homeowners and cooks, these dings, scrapes, bumps and gouges are a plus, showing signs of experience and life. For others, even a few fingerprints and scratches from skillets or sauté pans will be major flaws.

Wood

PRO: The most frequently used wood for countertops is hard sugar maple. Its color is pleasing and versatile. Beech is another favored material, with a more golden tone. These woods come in a variety of widths and lengths. Wood adds warmth and a pleasing texture to kitchens. Many people like the look of butcherblock — to others it looks dated and clichéd.

CON: When water is left on a wood countertop, it will usually penetrate the wood and stain it. Must be treated with an oil-based cleaner every six months, depending on use. Will burn or singe from very hot pans or baking trays.

Marble

PRO: Wide range of beautiful colors, textures, patterns. Your piece of marble is a one-of-a-kind, earth-made work of art. Marble has been used for centuries, and it is clearly very durable. Unusual colors include rose, salmon, celadon, dark green, black, ivory, deep brown, white with unusual yellow and green veining, black with flashes of mica and minerals—all with black or white graining. Finish can be either glossy or satiny. Comes in a range of sizes. Marble can be finished with bullnose, square, or other edging. Often an attractive inset into a wood counter.

CON: May be expensive. You may have to wait to get just the color or slab you want. Patterns of large, bold, colorful veins can be too insistent. Can crack or stain. Large slabs may have some weaknesses. Can be a little risky with an inexperienced installer. Well-sealed and finished, and re-buffed over time, it should perform well. Also note that you cannot cut on marble — it will ruin your knives and the marble may get scratched.

Laminates and Solid Surface

PRO: They're hard-wearing, usually low-cost, impervious to stains, nicks, and gouges. Available in a broad and versatile range of colors, finishes, and patterns.

CON: Possibly visible seams. Purists believe that synthetic countertops may be very practical but they don't gain character or charm with use, have no true depth of color, and often lack individuality. You won't see wine stains or other mementos of festive occasions. While some find the unblemished surface pleasing, others bemoan its lack of real textural variation. Laminates will not reveal "signs of life," and many kitchen planners feel its plain surface lacks tactile pleasure.

Tile

PRO: Easy to install. Comes in the widest possible range of colors, sizes, patterns, images, surfaces, textures, and styles. Can easily be custom-made and custom-styled. Not expensive. Impervious to heat and wear. Old tiles found at salvage yards and flea markets can add great individuality to a kitchen counter. Consider mixing some vintage tiles with plainer new tiles. Installation is very cost effective.

CON: Visible grout may be a problem. Cleaning of the tiles is simple, but grout can stain and require attention. Worn grout should be replaced.

OPPOSITE In Terrence O'Flaherty's kitchen, beautifully marked white marble gives the room subtle patterning. Garden view adds pleasure.

BELOW White tiles are easy to style and clean. Kitchen: Scott Waterman and Brett Landenburger.

DAVID LEBOVITZ

Creating a new kitchen from three useless "utility" rooms was the first order of business when David Lebovitz, pastry cook at Chez Panisse, and his partner, interior designer Kip Turnquist, purchased a Victorian flat in San Francisco.

Working closely with architect Bob Glazier of Hill Architects, Palo Alto, they designed a large new kitchen equipped with a Wolf range, a Sub-Zero refrigerator/ freezer, a Bosch dishwasher, and a microwave (for steaming vegetables).

Lebovitz and Turnquist's kitchen has its fun side, too. Pine wall cabinets display a vibrant 1,000-piece collection of Fiesta ware. For dining *a deux*, they have an authentic fifties restaurant booth, with the original banquettes newly upholstered in indigo blue Naugahyde.

"It took a year and a lot of patience to finish the kitchen," said Lebovitz. "Now, everything we need for cooking is at hand. I can make a batch of cookies in five minutes. And the stainless-steel counters are a snap to clean."

Lebovitz and Turnquist wanted wide counters, a large custom-designed porcelain sink and easily accessible ingredient storage. They also selected a water-saving Bosch dishwasher with removable dish racks that make room for large and unwieldy pots and pans. They have recessed halogen task lighting over counters, with added fluorescent strips under and above the wall cabinets for extra light. Stainless-steel counters are ultra-wide.

"As a cook, I wanted to have a large expanse of work space," said Lebovitz. "When I'm making pie dough, puff pastry, or preserves, I can set out all the ingredients while I'm working."

All of the lower shelves are equipped with pullout shelves for storing large baking sheets, bowls, and odd-sized baking equipment. Lebovitz chose plain matte-finish pine cabinets with clear glass fronts to house his twelve-year-old collection

of colorful Fiesta ware. "I found the ready-made cabinets at IKEA in Burbank," said Lebovitz, who drove a U-Haul to Southern California to pick them up.

Here are some of the tips he's learned from experience:

SIZE Make your kitchen as large as space and money allow. It's the most used room in the house and should be as pleasant and comfortable as possible.

EQUIPMENT Decide which fixtures and equipment you will *really* use and spend money on those items. If you love baking, invest in a good convection oven. If you enjoy making bread, a large and powerful mixer and a wide counter will make your job easier. Such items as wok-burners, smoking cabinets, and wine cabinets may look good (and some people do use them), but they're expensive and may not prove useful.

SAFETY Don't put your fire extinguisher next to the stove! If there's a fire, you won't be able to get to it.

LIGHTING Plan lighting thoroughly and carefully at the beginning of a remodel, since it is expensive and difficult to add later.

MATERIALS Use countertop materials that are smooth and seamless. This makes for easy maintenance. Stainless steel is durable, goes with any decor, is practically indestructible, and never goes out of style. Get a professional sheetmetal worker to do the fabrication and installation. Some contractors have little experience with stainless steel. You could ask your local restaurant for a recommendation.

FIXTURES Surgical and institutional fixtures for your kitchen sink are both practical and generally compatible with almost any decor. High faucets and deep sinks are great for cleaning large pots and sheet pans. The oversized handles on surgical faucets can be operated with forearms when your hands are sticky.

PROXIMITY Put your primary work spaces immediately next to the sink and stove. These are the two places where you spend most of your time preparing and cooking, so having everything close by will make work a lot easier and more efficient.

ABOVE In their Upper Haight kitchen, pastry cook David Lebovitz and designer Kip Turnquist chose easy-to-maintain stainless-steel counters and restaurant-worthy appliances.

OPPOSITE David Lebovitz set up his own "diner" in the kitchen, complete with banquettes and Fiesta dinnerware. A happy morning sight!

CHUCK'S CHECKLIST FOR KITCHEN EQUIPMENT

Getting your kitchen up to speed means buying the basics first. Inspect all utensils and appliances for fine craftsmanship. Be a picky consumer.

Chuck Williams founded Williams-Sonoma in the small, picturesque town of Sonoma, in Northern California, three decades ago. Williams-Sonoma is now a mega-company with stores throughout the country, and the best kitchen catalogue for cooks.

Chuck has kitchen equipment figured out — because he is an enthusiastic and lifelong cook. You might think that, as a big cheese at San Francisco-based Williams Sonoma, he would have a kitchen full of all the latest gadgets, fancy machines, and dozens of pots, pans, gizmos, and gear. In fact, Chuck is an unpretentious kitchen purist who dislikes gimmicks and prefers simple, honest knives, everyday tools, and classic hands-on methods. He believes in buying top-quality equipment (like the Dualit toaster—built like a Mack truck—and hardworking All-Clad pans) and using them for a lifetime.

Getting your kitchen up to speed can be so much easier if you know which basics you should buy first. Here are the solid, useful tools and cooking equipment you will use every day or every week. Collect them over time—and throw in some vintage tools and charity-shop finds so that your kitchen doesn't have that never-used, instant-decor look. You'll want to add specialized pieces if you're a whiz at pastry making, whipping up house-made candy or chocolate confections, or bread baking.

Chuck Williams knows—from decades of cooking, hunting all over the world for tools-of-the-trade, and customer feedback—that every cook is very opinionated about the right utensils, pots, grills, knives,

and pans. For some, nonstick pots are the ne plus ultra. Other cooks find them just to newfangled. Many appreciate mixers and blenders. Others love painstaking hands-on cooking, with nothing electrical, thank you. But everyone will agree: start with the best-quality knives and sturdy equipment. And use only the freshest ingredients.

Chuck's Ten Essentials

I. 6- or 8-quart saucepot—for everything from pasta to soup

II. Small skillets—for many uses, including browning, frying

III. 3- or 5-quart sauté pan

IV. Regular or oval baking dish

V. 3 1/2- or 4-inch paring knife—for fruit and vegetables

VI. 8-inch chef's knife—a handy tool that will do everything from chopping herbs or carrots to slicing meat

VII. A food processor. It can do everything—fast and efficiently — from chopping vegetables to giving pastry or batter a good consistency

VIII. Measuring cups, liquid and dry measure

IX. Measuring spoons

X. A cutting board

OPPOSITE Chefs Nancy Oakes and Bruce Aidells like sturdy, no-nonsense appliances and equipment. Their capacious bowls, well-crafted pots and pans, and hefty countertops are made to last for decades-and take hard wear.

CUTLERY

3½- or 4-inch paring knife
8-inch chef (chopping) knife
Serrated bread knife
Knife block to protect knife blades and keep them on the counter, at the ready

COOKWARE

1- or 1½-quart saucepan
2½-quart saucepan
8- or 9-inch omelet pan
3- or 5-quart sauté pan
6- or 8-quart saucepot
Stockpot
Roasting rack
Medium-sized roasting pan
Steaming basket
Teakettle

BAKEWARE

Flour sifter
Cake pan
Muffin tin
9-inch pie tin
9-inch springform pan
Cookie sheet
Cooling racks
Pastry scraper
Rolling pin
Round baking dish
Three mixing bowls, in various sizes
Rectangular or oval baking dish

TOOLS FOR COOKS

Stainless-steel spatula
Pastry brush
Stainless-steel tongs
Rubber spatula for scraping
Two all-purpose stainless-steel spoons—one slotted, one plain
Two or three wooden spoons in different styles—small, large, in different shapes, plus with long and short handles
Strainer
Small spatula or butter spreader
Cutting board
Grater, shredder
Vegetable peeler
Both liquid and dry measuring cups
A collection of measuring spoons
Whisk
Heavy-duty can opener
Masher or potato ricer
Timer (unless you have one on your stove)
Instant-read thermometer
Oven thermometer
Bulb baster (for roasted meats and poultry)
Well-made kitchen scissors with good grips
Lemon reamer
Plain, simple potholders (no fashion statements or trendy designs)
Classic white cotton or cotton/linen kitchen towels and glass cloths

ELECTRONIC APPLIANCES

Citrus juicer
Coffeemaker
Food processor (if you're going to do a lot of cooking and entertaining)
Electric mixer (if you plan to do a lot of baking)

OPPOSITE Stainless steel endures and takes the heat. Its sheen can be quite alluring.

BELOW In Christopher Bigelow's kitchen: retro appliances.

FINAL THOUGHTS ON RENOVATIONS

Ask any brave soul who has remodeled a kitchen, and they'll say that demolishing and rebuilding take commitment and patience.

Transforming an outdated, non-functioning, dark, and dull kitchen into a light-filled, efficient, modern wonder is not a piece of cake. Choosing the marble and selecting drawer pulls and a new stove is the fun part. Construction is another matter.

But of course, every new kitchen begins with a dream — and a hope and a prayer.

Then there are all the kitchen designs and materials to choose, colors to agonize over, marbles to compare, woods to touch and inspect. Should it be a vintage stove or a gleaming new one? What about those copper hoods? Will antique lighting fixtures cast adequate light and pass code? Can salvaged doors and faucets work in the new kitchen configuration?

Stung by the remodeling bug, you spend days looking for just the right door pulls, some witty handles, the perfect frosted glass for those upper cabinets. Should the marble counter be simply honed to satiny perfection? Which flooring requires no upkeep? Where can you display your silver collection, Fiesta, books, and glass?

And then the work begins in earnest.

Every homeowner who has gone through a kitchen remodel will tell you about the week they couldn't cook because the kitchen was demolished — and just when they thought they'd be giving a celebratory dinner party, there was no water for a fortnight. They'll recount battlefield stories of perfectionistic and painfully slow craftsmen, of trucks tearing up the driveway, and tell you about the morning when they simply couldn't stand the dirt and dust another minute and checked into a hotel.

Kitchen renovators will recount the time they found chunks of plaster in their shoes, or the afternoon they discovered they had dry rot, termites, beetles, antiquated wiring, fire-hazard ceilings, and a crumbling chimney. Renovating may mean nasty surprises. Dining out every night because the new stove hasn't arrived can become tedious. Then again, you'll make lots of new friends. Architects, designers, hardware-store assistants, floor sanders, painters, plumbers, lumberyard helpers, and cabinetmakers will all know everything about your kitchen — and your personal life.

Of course, kitchen remodeling veterans tell you all their horror stories in the comfort of their beautiful new kitchen. Sunshine pours in through the handsome new windows. Marjoram and fragrant basil flourish on the windowsill. Salmon sizzles on the new grill. Pasta bubbles on the new stove. The new dining table is welcoming and the kitchen feels friendly, comfortable, and a dream come true. Which makes savoring the nightmarish stories just so much sweeter.

ABOVE Tall windows draw light and air from the Napa Valley into this sunny kitchen. Architect: Rob Wilkinson.

OPPOSITE This Santa Monica kitchen, with its modern simplicity, has easy access to other rooms. Architect: Michael Sant.

DREAM KITCHENS

My ideal kitchen must have a beautiful view out the window — of San Francisco Bay, Oaxaca, or the south of France. My requirements are simple: good sharp knives, clean water, serviceable pots and pans, a fireplace, a good wine cellar, beautiful china and glassware, a dining table, and people I love to cook for.

Reed Hearon
Chef/owner
Rose Pistola
San Francisco

The ideal kitchen would have a long wooden table large enough to seat up to sixteen people. I like a clay-pot cooker, a gas burner for a wok, a tandoori oven, a marble counter for rolling pastry. Another essential for me is a good, industrial-strength toaster for making toasted tomato sandwiches — which I eat daily.

Todd Humphries
Executive chef
Campton Place Restaurant,
Campton Place Hotel
San Francisco

My must-have ingredients for a happy, fun, and practical kitchen would include All-Clad pans, six gas burners, wine for sipping, large counters, fresh fruit trees, kosher salt, a movable cutting board, boiling tap water, high-quality olive oils and vinegars, cracked pepper, a handy herb garden, and good ventilation.

Michael Mina
Executive chef
Aqua and Charles Nob Hill
restaurants
San Francisco

A well-designed kitchen should have crisp white walls, a red island stove that everyone can cook around, a wood-burning oven, and a sound system playing classical music. I like to have menus from top chefs framed on the walls. It keeps me inspired and on my toes!

Fabrice Canelle
Chef de cuisine
Moose's
San Francisco

OPPOSITE Designer Julie Atwood built a half wall to conceal the working kitchen. Everything is at hand — but not always on view.

Designing, equiping, and stocking and decorating a kitchen — and your house — is much more than just shopping for basics today. Stores throughout California offer the widest possible range of fabrics, tableware, pots and pans, cabinetry, decor, appliances, and glassware — along with one-of-a-kind, artist-made ceramic designs, linens, vases, electronic gear, and furniture. To get the most style in your house — and your kitchen — seek out unusual antiques, quirky collections, inspired artists and craftspeople, and passionate designers. *Diane Dorrans Saeks*

LOS ANGELES

You must have wheels, of course, to go design shopping in Los Angeles. On weekends, flea markets in Pasadena and Long Beach are lively. Best centers of style include shops on North Robertson Avenue, Melrose Avenue (the western end), along La Brea, Larchmont, and out in Santa Monica. But part of the fun of shopping for furniture, linen sheets, silk pillows, fabrics or antiques is screeching to a halt in front of a new store on an as-yet undiscovered avenue.

AMERICAN RAG CIE MAISON ET CAFE
148 S. La Brea Avenue
(Also in San Francisco)
The home of California/French style with Provençal pottery, books, French kitchenware — plus a tiny cafe.

ANICHINI
466 N. Robertson Boulevard
Bedroom glamour and luxury. Gorgeous silk-bound cashmere blankets, linen sheets, jacquard weave throws and heirloom blankets.

PAMELA BARSKY
100 N. La Cienega Boulevard
(Beverly Connection)
Changing range of decorative objects, tabletop decor with fresh wit.

BLACKMAN-CRUZ
800 N. La Cienega Boulevard
Influential and addictive. Stylish and often odd twentieth-century objects and furniture. Clocks, architectural fragments. A big favorite with stylists, Hollywood set designers, designers.

BOOK SOUP
8818 Sunset Boulevard,
West Hollywood
My great favorite. Must-visit bookstore, with all-day and midnight browsing. Walls of design, architecture, and photography books. Open-air magazine stand has all the international design magazines.

CITY ANTIQUES
8444 Melrose Avenue
A fine source for eighteenth-through twentieth-century furniture, some by admired but slightly obscure designers. An influential look.

NANCY CORZINE
8747 Melrose Avenue
(To the trade only.) Edited, elegant, suavely updated classic furnishings. Outstanding Italian fabric collection.

DIALOGICA
8304 Melrose Avenue
Smooth contemporary furniture.

DIAMOND FOAM & FABRIC
611 S. La Brea Avenue
Design insiders' favorite
Long a secret source for well-priced fabrics, Jason Asch's bustling treasure house offers the added benefit of off-the-rack basics textiles, plus linen, chintz, silk, and damask shopping.

RANDY FRANKS
8448 Melrose Place
One-of-a-kind furniture. New designers.

HOLLYHOCK
214 N. Larchmont Boulevard
A cozy, elegant look. Fabrics, furniture, and decorative accessories for house and garden.

INDIGO SEAS
123 N. Robertson Boulevard
Noel Coward anyone? Lynn von Kersting's madly energized style: part exotic Caribbean Colonial, part south of France, part Olde Idealized England. Sofas, soaps.

LA MAISON DU BAL
705 N. Harper Avenue
Exquisite antique and vintage textiles, idiosyncratic lighting, antique French furniture. Friendly atmosphere.

LIEF
8922 Beverly Boulevard
Elegant pared-down Gustavian antiques and simple Scandinavian Biedermeier are a refreshing change from Fine French Furniture.

MODERNICA
7366 Beverly Boulevard
Modernist furniture, focusing on twenties to sixties. Reproductions.

RICHARD MULLIGAN–SUNSET COTTAGE
8157 Sunset Boulevard
(To the trade only: 213-650-8660.) With your decorator in tow, get seduced by the Mulligans' chic country vision. Richard and Mollie have star power and a loyal following among Hollywood designers and celebs. Antique and vintage

country-style antiques.
Beautifully finessed painted
reproductions and collectible
one-of-a-kind lamps.

ODALISQUE
7278 Beverly Boulevard
Stars come here to hang out
among the silks and pillows.
Finest embroidered antique
fabrics and glorious vintage
textiles. One-of-a-kind pillows
and draperies made from
ecclesiastical, operatic fabrics.
The owners' obsession and
admiration for old fabrics
is catching.

PACIFIC DESIGN CENTER
8687 Melrose Avenue
To-the-trade showrooms such as
Mimi London, Donghia, Randolph
& Hein, and Kneedler-Fauchere
and Snaidero present the finest
fabrics, furniture, lighting, rugs,
hardware, reproductions, decorative accessories, fixtures.

RIZZOLI BOOKSTORE
9501 Wilshire Boulevard
(Also in Santa Monica)
Top-notch selection of design
and architecture books. Linger
among the design books stacks.
Open late.

ROSE TARLOW—
MELROSE HOUSE
8454 Melrose Place
Rose Tarlow has a great sense of
furniture scale and an exquisite
understanding of luxury, elegance,
line, and grace. A certain Conti-
nental/English sensibility and glamour in her furniture collection.

RUSSELL SIMPSON COMPANY
8109 Melrose Avenue
Bret Witke and Diane Rosenstein
sell furniture from the forties and
fifties. Eames, Jacobsen, Saarinen,
Robsjohn-Gibbings—like that.

SILK TRADING COMPANY
353-351 S. La Brea Avenue
Super selection of fabrics—silk
and everything else. Custom-
made pillows, helpful swatch
collections. Excellent prices
and choices.

W ANTIQUES AND
EXCENTRICITIES
8925 Melrose Avenue
Melissa Deitz's charming, jam-
packed shop sells everything
from eighteenth-century gilded
chairs to birdcage-shaped chan-
deliers, chinoiseries, fountains,
urns, art deco furniture. It's one-
of-a-kind and ever-changing.

SAN FRANCISCO

My favorite shopping streets:
Fillmore, Hayes, Brady, Post,
Sutter, Sacramento, Polk, Gough,
Union. For top-notch stores
explore Fillmore Street from
Pacific Avenue to Bush Street, and
Post Street from Union Square
to Montgomery Street.

AGRARIA
1051 Howard Street
Telephone 415-863-7700 for
an appointment. A longtime
favorite. Maurice Gibson and
Stanford Stevenson's classic
potpourri and soaps are tops.
(Also sold at Gump's.)

ARCH
407 Jackson Street
Architect Susan Colliver's colorful shop sells serious supplies
for designers, architects, and
artists. Excellent ranges of
papers, pencils, frames.

BELL'OCCHIO
8 Brady Street
Tiny but worth a detour, Claudia
Schwartz and Toby Hanson's
whimsical boutique offers
hand-painted ribbons, French
silk flowers. Trips to Paris and
Florence produce charming
tableware, antiques, and retro-
chic Italian and Parisian soaps
and face powders.

GORDON BENNETT
2102 Union Street
Garden style throughout the
seasons. Vases, plants, books,
candles, decoupage plates, and
tools. (Ask the owner to explain
the name—and to introduce his
handsome poodles.)

BLOOMERS
2975 Washington Street
Patric Powell's fragrant domain.
Bloomers blooms all seasons
with the freshest cut flowers
and orchids. Walls of vases,
French ribbons and baskets.
Nothing frou-frou or fussy
here—just nature's bounty
and beauty.

VIRGINIA BREIER
3091 Sacramento Street
A gallery for contemporary and
traditional American crafts.

BRITEX
146 Geary Street
Growing home design sections.
Action-central for thousands of
fabrics. World-class selections of
classic and unusual furnishing
textiles, trims, notions.

BROWN DIRT COWBOYS
2418 Polk Street
Painted and refurbished
furniture, housewares.

BULGARI
237 Post Street
Browse in the superb upstairs
silver department . . . it's heaven
. . . then lavish something golden
and decorative upon yourself.

CANDELIER
60 Maiden Lane
Wade Benson's virtuoso store
for candles and all their
accoutrements. Superb collection of candlesticks, books,
and tabletop decor.

CARTIER
231 Post Street
Elegant selection of crystal,
vases, porcelain.

CLERVI MARBLE
221 Bayshore Boulevard
Eighty-year-old source for
noble and beautiful natural
stones—marble, onyx,
travertine and more. Countertops and tabletops.

COLUMBINE DESIGN
1541 Grant Avenue
On a pioneering bock of North Beach, Kathleen Dooley sells fresh flowers and gifts along with shells, graphic framed butterflies, bugs, and beetles.

THE COTTAGE TABLE COMPANY
550 18th Street
Tony Cowan custom-makes heirloom-quality hardwood tables to order. Shipping available. Catalogue.

DE VERA
334 Gough Street
A must-visit store. Objets trouves, sculpture. Remarkable, original small-scale finds and original designs by Federico de Vera.

DE VERA GLASS
384 Hayes Street
A mesmerizing gallery of vibrant glass objects by contemporary American artists, along with Venetian and Scandinavian classics. Ted Muehling jewelry.

EARTHSAKE
2076 Chestnut Street
(Also in the Embarcadero Center, Berkeley, and Palo Alto)
Earth-friendly stores with attractive tableware, furniture, unbleached bed linens and towels, politically correct beds, vases of recycled glass, candles.

F. DORIAN
388 Hayes Street
Treasures galore—at excellent prices. Contemporary accessories, folk arts, and antiques.

FILLAMENTO
2185 Fillmore Street
For more than a decade, a must for design aficionados. Go-go owner Iris Fuller fills three floors with colorful, style-conscious furniture, tableware, glass, toiletries, and gifts. Iris is always first with new designers' works and supports local talent, including Ann Gish, Annieglass and Cyclamen. Frames, lamps, linens, beds, and partyware.

FIORIDELLA
1920 Polk Street
Flower-lovers alert: For more than sixteen years, Jean Thompson and Barbara Belloli have been offering the most beautiful flowers and plants. Exclusive selection of decorative accessories and versatile vases. Mexican folk crafts, orchids, furniture—in a luscious interior.

FLAX
1699 Market Street
Tasty, tempting selections of papers, lighting, tabletop accessories, boxes, art books, furnishings. One-stop shopping for art supplies. Catalogue.

FORZA
1742 Polk Street
Handcrafted furniture, candles, accessories with a certain rustic elegance. Great aesthetic.

STANLEE R. GATTI FLOWERS
Fairmont Hotel, Nob Hill
Vibrant outpost for fresh flowers, Agraria potpourri, vases, and candles.

GEORGE
2411 California Street
Pet heaven. Style for dogs, including designs by both Todd Oldham and Tom Bonauro for canine charms, toys, pillows, bowls and accessories. Best dog treats: whole-grain biscuits.

GREEN WORLD MERCANTILE
2340 Polk Street
Serious owners sell earth-friendly housewares, clothing, gardening equipment, plants, books, and unpretentious decorative accessories.

GUMP'S
135 Post Street
Genius Geraldine Stutz has dreamed up the new Gump's—with beautifully displayed crafts, fine art, Orient-inspired accessories, plus tip-top names in silver, crystal, and elegant linens and tableware. Recent refurbishing makes the store an essential stop. Be sure to visit the silver, Treillage, and decorative glass departments. Catalogue.

ED HARDY SAN FRANCISCO
188 Henry Adams Street
In an elegant Palladian-style villa, Hardy offers a delicious array of Continental, Asian, English, and American antiques. Most tempting: painted furniture, screens, gilded chairs, and handsome garden antiques.

HERMES
212 Stockton Street
Gallop up the limestone stairs for tableware, silk and decorative accessories—then reward yourself with a silk tie or scarf.

RICHARD HILKERT BOOKS
333 Hayes Street
Hushed, like a private library. Decorators and the book-addicted telephone Richard and Manuel to order out-of-print style books and new design books. Browsing here on Saturday afternoons is especially pleasant.

INDIGO V
1352 Castro Street
Diane's fresh flowers are quirky, original. A year-round favorite.

IN MY DREAMS
1300 Pacific
Jewelry designer Harry Fireside's dreamy shop for antiques, topiaries, and Chinese lanterns.

JAPONESQUE
824 Montgomery Street
Aesthete Koichi Hara demonstrates his appreciation of tradition, harmony, simplicity, refined beauty, and humble materials. Japanese graphics, sculpture, glass, furniture. Timeless and tranquil gallery.

JUICY NEWS
2453 Fillmore Street
The best local haunt for every possible design, architecture and style magazine—and fresh fruit juices.

KRIS KELLY
One Union Square
Selections of beds, fine linens, and table linens.

SUE FISHER KING
3067 Sacramento Street
Sue King's Italian, French, and English crystal, platters, bed linens, and tableware are the chicest and prettiest. Luxurious blankets, plus accessories, books, soaps, furniture, and silk and cashmere throws.

LIMN
290 Townsend Street
Lively stop on Saturday afternoons. Contemporary furniture, accessories, and lighting by over 300 manufacturers. Well-priced, take-out collections along with Philippe Starck, Andree Putman, and Mathieu & Ray for Ecart, plus top Northern California talent. Ceramics by Cyclamen. Visit the new gallery behind the store.

DAVID LUKE & ASSOCIATE
773 14th Street
Antiques, vintage tableware, vintage furniture, old garden ornaments—many from the estates of England. (David's boxer, Baby, is the associate.)

MAC
1543 Grant Avenue
Chris Ospital's trend-setting salon sells style inspiration. Stop and chat: Talent-spotter Chris knows what's new, when, where.

MACY'S
Union Square
The Cellar has an impressive and thorough selection of kitchen equipment, tools, tableware. Furniture and accessories floors display popular selections of furnishings. Interior Design Department has designers available to assist with decorating. New: simply elegant Calvin Klein Home.

MAISON D'ETRE
32 South Park
In a new Toby Levy-designed building, ever-changing collections of vintage furniture, lighting, handblown glass bowls, candlesticks, vases, candles. Presented with spirit.

MIKE FURNITURE
Corner of Fillmore and Sacramento streets
With design directed by Mike Moore and partner Mike Thackar, this spacious, sunny store sells updated furniture classics-with-a-twist by Beverly and other manufacturers. Good design here is very accessible. One-stop shopping for fast-delivery sofas, fabrics, lamps, tables, fabrics, accessories.

NAOMI'S ANTIQUES TO GO
1817 Polk Street
Collectors throng here for art pottery! Bauer and Fiesta, of course, plus historic studio pottery. American railroad, airline, luxury liner, and bus depot china.

NEST
2300 Fillmore Street
Where a neighborhood pharmacy stood for decades Marcella Madsen and Judith Gilman have feathered a new Nest. Seductive treasures include books, silk flowers, rustic antiques, prints, sachets, and pillows.

PAINT EFFECTS
2426 Fillmore Street
Paint experts Sheila Rauch and partner Patricia Orlando have a loyal following for their range of innovative paint finishes and tools. Hands-on paint technique classes by Lesley Ruda, along with materials for gilding, limning, crackle glazing, decoupage, stenciling, and other decorative finishes.

PAXTON GATE
1204 Stevenson Street
Authentic butterfly nets, anyone? Peter Kline and Sean Quigley's gardening store offers uncommon plants (such as sweetly scented Buddha's Hand citron trees) plus orchids, vases, and hand-forged tools.

POLANCO
393 Hayes Street
For certain uplift, see these superbly presented Mexican fine arts, photography, and crafts. Museum curator Elsa Cameron says you can't find better in Mexico.

POLO RALPH LAUREN
Crocker Galleria, corner of Post and Kearney streets
Ralph Lauren's striking new emporium purveys the complete Home collection. Best-quality furniture, linens, and the trappings of fine rooms, country houses.

PORTOBELLO
3915 24th Street
A tiny treasure. Old furniture in new guises, kilims, decorative objects.

POTTERY BARN
Throughout California
The San Francisco–based company has stores all over the country, including New York. New full-service design stores offer furniture, rugs, draperies, special orders. Practical, well-priced home style. Excellent basics. Classic, accessible design. Catalogue.

RAYON VERT
3187 16th Street
Worth the trek to the Mission. Floral designer Kelly Kornegay's garden of earthly delights! Porcelains, flowers, artifacts, glasses, architectural fragments in a full-tilt, all-out, humble-chic setting.

RH
2506 Sacramento Street
Rick Herbert's sunny garden and tableware store has beeswax candles, dinnerware by Sebastapol artist Aletha Soule. Inspiring selection of sconces, cachepots, vases. Topiaries, too.

RIZZOLI BOOKS
117 Post Street
New, next to Gump's. Elegant book-lovers' paradise. Outstanding collection of design, architecture and photography books. Cafe.

SAN FRANCISCO DESIGN CENTER GALLERIA AND SHOWPLACE
Henry Adams Street
It is wise to come to this South of Market design center with your decorator. A professional's eye can lead you to the best sofas, trims, silks, accessories, fabrics. These to-the-trade-only buildings, along with Showplace West and other nearby showrooms, offer top-of-the-line furniture, fabrics, and furnishings. Randolph & Hein, Kneedler-Fauchere, Sloan Miyasato, Shears & Window, Clarence House, Palacek, Brunschwig & Fils, Schumacher, Therien Studio,

McRae Hinckley, Donghia, Summit Furniture, Enid Ford and Houles are personal favorites. Also in the neighborhood: Therien & Co (Scandinavian, Continental and English antiques) and the handsome outpost of Ed Hardy San Francisco (eclectic antiques and worldly reproductions).

SATIN MOON FABRICS
32 Clement Street
Twenty-four-year-old store sells a well-edited collection of decorating linens, trims, chintzes, and well-priced fabrics.

SCHEUER LINENS
340 Sutter Street
Longtime, well-focused store for fine-quality bed linens, blankets. This staff facilitates custom orders particularly well.

SHABBY CHIC
3075 Sacramento Street
(Also in Los Angeles)
Specializes in chairs and sofas with comfortable airs and loose-fitting slipcovers.

SLIPS
1534 Grant Avenue
Sami Rosenzweig's spirit lives on. Custom-made slipcovers for chairs and sofas, plus draperies, decorations, ottomans.

SUE FISHER KING HOME AT WILKES BASHFORD
375 Sutter Street
Glamour galore. Sue's dynamic vision shines with tableware, accessories, furniture, and special objets d'art from Italy, France, London. Books.

TIFFANY & CO
350 Post Street
Try on a diamond ring, a Paloma Picasso necklace, then head upstairs to the venerated crystal, china, and silver departments. Ask about Elsa Peretti's classic glasses, bowls, and silver.

WILLIAMS-SONOMA
150 Post Street
Everything for kitchens. Bustling flagship for the Williams-Sonoma cookware empire. Stores throughout the state, including Corte Madera, Palo Alto, Rodeo Drive, Pasadena. Delicacies. Outstanding basics for serious and dilettante cooks. Outstanding catalogues.

WILLIAM STOUT ARCHITECTURAL BOOKS
804 Montgomery Street
Architect Bill Stout's chock-a-block bookstore specializes in basic and obscure twentieth-century architecture publications, along with new and out-of-print design and garden books. Catalogue.

WORLDWARE
336 Hayes Street
Enduring classic design. Shari Sant's eco-store sells cozy unbleached sheets and blankets, vintage-wear, and such delights as patchwork pillows, deluxe candles. Interiors crafted by Dan Plummer from recycled materials. Catalogue.

ZINC DETAILS
1905 Fillmore Street
The vibrant Zinc Details shop has a cult following. Architect-designed and handcrafted furniture, lighting. Extraordinary hand-blown glass vases by international artists. Domain of Wendy Nishimura and Vasilios Kiniris. (No, they don't sell anything made of zinc.)

ZONAL HOME INTERIORS
568 Hayes Street
Visit Hayes Valley and Russell Pritchard's pioneering gallery store of one-of-a-kind rustic furniture and decorative objects. He made the patina of rust and the textures of loving use fashionable. Old Americana at its best.

BERKELEY, ELMWOOD

Much of the design store action here is focused on wonderfully revived Fourth Street. We recommend a detour to Cafe Fanny, the Acme Bread bakery, Chez Panisse, and shops in the Elmwood.

BERKELEY MILLS
2830 Seventh Street
Handcrafted fine Japanese- and Mission-influenced furniture. Blends the best of old-world craftsmanship with high-tech. All built to order. Catalogue.

BUILDERS BOOKSOURCE
1817 Fourth Street
Well-displayed design, architecture, gardening, and building books.

CAMPS AND COTTAGES
2109 Virginia Street
First lunch at Chez Panisse or Berkeley's beloved Cheese Board, then walk here for a visit. This little shop sells charming homey furniture and low-key accessories. Owner Molly Hyde English has perfect pitch for Adirondack styles.

CYCLAMEN
1825 Eastshore Highway
Restless designer Julie Sanders's colorful ceramics seconds— with barely discernible flaws— are available at the factory store, by appointment. Broad range of designs. (Her vibrant Cyclamen Studio designs are featured at Fillamento, Henri Bendel.)

ELIKA'S PAPERS
1801 Fourth Street
Eriko Kurita's eight-year old shop specializes in Japanese handmade papers. The store custom-makes stationery, albums, frames, paper wall-hangings, decorative boxes, sketchbooks. The most intriguing papers are made from mulberry bark. Papers can be used for making lampshades, window shades, screens, even wallpaper.

THE GARDENER
1836 Fourth Street
Pioneer Alta Tingle's brilliant, inspired garden store sells tools, vases, books, tables, chairs, tableware, paintings, clothing, and food for nature-lovers—whether they have a garden or are just dreaming. Consistently original, classic style.

LIGHTING STUDIO
1808 Fourth Street
Lighting design services. Contemporary lamps.

SUR LA TABLE
1806 Fourth Street
Outpost of the twenty-four-year-old Seattle cookware company but feels entirely original. In a 5,000-square-foot "warehouse," the shop stocks every imaginable goodie, gadget, tool, utensil, plate, machine, and kitchen decoration for serious and dilettante cooks. Catalogue, too.

TAIL OF THE YAK
2632 Ashby Avenue
Chic partners Alice Hoffman Erb and Lauren Adams Allard have created a magical store that is always worth the trip—across the bay or across the country. Decorative accessories, wedding gifts, Mexican furniture, fabrics, ribbons, notecards, Lauren's books, tableware, and antique jewelry.

ERICA TANOV
1627 San Pablo Avenue
Antiques. The place for pajamas, romantic bed accessories. Erica's lace-edged sheets and shams, and linen duvet covers are quietly luxurious. (Drop in to Kermit Lynch Wine Merchants, Acme Bread, and Cafe Fanny just up the street.)

ZIA
1310 Tenth Street
Collin Smith's sun-filled gallery-store offers a changing variety of hands-on furniture designs and art.

THE PHOENIX
Highway 1
An enduring store where you can linger for hours. Collections of handcrafted decorative objects, wind chimes, glass, books, sculpture, jewelry, hand-knit sweaters by Kaffe Fassett (who grew up in Big Sur), and toys. Coastal views from all windows. Be sure to walk downstairs. Crystals, soothing music, and hand-made objects are on all sides. The sixties never truly left Big Sur—thank goodness.

SAMANTHA COLE
1436 Burlingame Avenue
Smoothly executed traditional style with a light hand. Decor for comfortable interiors.

GARDENHOUSE
1129 Howard Avenue
Topiaries, garden ornaments, beautifully presented decorative accessories.

CARMEL BAY COMPANY
Corner of Ocean and Lincoln
Tableware, books, glassware, furniture, prints.

FRANCESCA VICTORIA
250 Crossroads Boulevard
Decorative accessories for garden and home. Fresh style.

LUCIANO ANTIQUES
San Carlos and Fifth streets
Cosmopolitan antiques. Wander through the vast rooms—to view furniture, lighting, sculpture, and handsome reproductions.

PLACES IN THE SUN
Dolores Avenue, near Ocean Avenue
Decor from sun-splashed climes. Provençal tables, Mexican candlesticks, colorful fabrics.

HEALDSBURG

JIMTOWN STORE
6706 State Highway 128
Drive or bike to J. Carrie Brown and John Werner's friendly country store in the Alexander Valley. The Mercantile & Exchange vintage Americana is cheerful and very well-priced. Comestibles.

MENLO PARK

MILLSTREET
1131 Chestnut Street
Objects of desire. Continental antiques, Ann Gish bed linens and silks, Tuscan pottery, tapestries, orchids, mirrors, botanical prints, silk and cashmere throws.

MENDOCINO

THE GOLDEN GOOSE
Main Street
An enduring favorite. Superb linens, antiques, tableware, overlooking the ocean. For more than a decade, the most stylish store in Mendocino. (When in Mendocino, be sure to make a dinner reservation at Cafe Beaujolais.)

WILKESSPORT
10466 Lansing Street
In addition to nifty sportswear, Wilkes Bashford offers David Luke garden antiques, crafts of the region, and paintings.

MILL VALLEY

CAPRICORN ANTIQUES & COOKWARE
100 Throckmorton Avenue
This quiet, reliable store seems to have been here forever. Basic cookware, along with antique tables, chests, and cupboards.

PULLMAN & CO
108 Throckmorton Street
Style inspiration. Understated but luxurious bed linens (the standouts are those by Ann Gish), along with furniture, frames, tableware, and accessories.

SMITH & HAWKEN
35 Corte Madera
The original. Superb nursery (begun under horticulturist Sarah Hammond's superb direction) and store. Everything for gardens. Also in San Francisco, Berkeley, Palo Alto, Los Gatos, Santa Rosa, and points beyond. Catalogues.

SUMMER HOUSE GALLERY
21 Throckmorton Street
Impossible to leave empty-handed. Artist-crafted accessories and (to order) comfortable sofas and chairs. Witty handcrafted frames, glassware, candlesticks, and colorful accessories. Slip-covered loveseats, vases, tables, gifts.

MONTECITO

PIERRE LAFOND/ WENDY FOSTER
516 San Ysidro Road
Handsomely displayed household furnishings, books, accessories, and South American and Malabar Coast furniture. Beautiful linens.

OAKLAND

MAISON D'ETRE
5330 College Avenue
Indoor/outdoor style. Engaging, eccentric, and whimsical decorative objects and furniture for rooms and gardens. Luscious.

PALO ALTO

BELL'S BOOKS
536 Emerson Street
An especially fine and scholarly selection of new, vintage and rare books on every aspect of gardens and gardening. Also literature, books on decorative arts, photography, cooking.

HILLARY THATZ
Stanford Shopping Center
An embellished view of the cozy interiors of England, as seen by Cheryl Driver. Traditional accessories, furniture, frames, and decorative objects. Beautifully presented garden furnishings.

POLO-RALPH LAUREN
Stanford Shopping Center
Just gets better and better — great design, no theme design. A spacious, gracious store. The expanding world imagined through Ralph Lauren's eyes. Outstanding selection of furniture, imaginary-heritage accessories, and quality housewares. Catalogue.

TURNER MARTIN
540 Emerson Street
David Turner and John Martin's enchanting one-of-a-kind style store/gallery.

PASADENA

HORTUS
284 E. Orange Grove Boulevard
Superbly selected perennials, antique roses, and a full nursery. Handsome collection of antique garden ornaments.

SAN ANSELMO

MODERN i
500 Red Hill Avenue
Worth the drive. Steven Cabella is passionate about Modernism and time-warp mid-century (1935-65) furnishings. Vintage furnishings, Eames chairs, furniture by architects, objects, and artwork. Located in a restored modernist architect's office building.

MANDERLEY

(By appointment: 415-472-6166)
Ronnie Wells's full-tilt glamorous silk shams, antique fabrics, and vintage pillows set trends. Outstanding throws in one-of-a-kind textiles.

ST. HELENA

BALE MILL CLASSIC COUNTRY FURNITURE
3431 North St. Helena Highway
Decorative and practical updated classic furniture in a wide range of styles. A favorite with decorators.

ST. HELENA ST. HELENA ANTIQUES
1231 Main Street
(Yes, the name is intentionally repetitious.) Rustic vintage wine paraphernalia, vintage furniture.

TANTAU
1220 Adams Street
Charming atmosphere. Decorative accessories, handpainted furniture, gifts.

TESORO
649 Main Street
Fresh-flower heaven. Topiaries, wreaths, vases, too.

TIVOLI
1432 Main Street
Tom Scheibal and partners have created another winner, an indoor/outdoor garden furniture and accessories store. Tables and chairs and useful occasional pieces are in iron, aluminum, concrete, and recycled redwood. Antique garden ornaments.

VANDERBILT & CO.
1429 Main Street
Stylish and colorful tableware, bed linens, books, glassware, Italian ceramics, accessories. A year-round favorite in the wine country.

SANTA MONICA

THOMAS CALLAWAY BENCHWORKS, INC.
2929 Nebraska Avenue
(By appointment only: 310-828-9379). High-energy interior designer Thomas Callaway offers star-quality armchairs, sofas, and ottomans with deep-down comfort and regal glamour. These are future heirlooms, very collectible.

HENNESSY & INGALLS
1254 Third Street, Promenade
Architects and designers flock to this bookstore, which specializes in the widest range of architectural books.

IRELAND-PAYS
2428 Main Street
Producer Kathryn Ireland and actress Amanda Pays (*Max Headroom*) created le style anglais for Anglophile Angelenos. Special pillows.

JASPER
1454 Fifth Street
Young interior designer Michael Smith's brilliant store and atelier. In a coolly elegant former art gallery, the high-ceilinged shop displays changing vignettes of antiques, linens, cashmeres, art glass, and Smith's own designs. Worth a detour.

ROOM WITH A VIEW
1600 Montana Avenue
Kitchenware, children's furnishings, and especially glamorous bed linens by the likes of Cocoon (silks), Bischoff, and Anichini.

SHABBY CHIC
1013 Montana Avenue
Yes, they still do great smooshy sofas, but they've also moved on to tailored upholstery and a new line of fabrics.

SONOMA

SLOAN AND JONES
147 E. Spain Street
Ann Jones and Sheelagh Sloan run and stock this splendid antiques and tableware store. Set in a fine old turn-of-the-century building, it's the place for country and porcelains, silverware, Asian vintage furniture, photography, linens, and garden accessories.

THE SONOMA COUNTRY STORE
165 West Napa Street
Ann Thornton's empire also includes her store at 3575 Sacramento Street, San Francisco. Decorative accessories, linens. Great for Christmas decorations and gifts.

VENICE

BOUNTIFUL
1335 Abbott Kinney Boulevard
(By appointment only: 310-450-3620.) Great Edwardian and Victorian painted furniture, lamps, old beds, quirky objets.

CATALOGUE PHOTOGRAPHS
Glassware on pages 111 and 112 by Annieglass, Inc., of Watsonville, California; everything else shown is by Williams-Sonoma/Pottery Barn.

Grey Crawford
1, 3, 12, 13, 42, 50, 103, 106

Laurie E. Dickson
6, 52, 108

Thomas Heinser
33, 97

Christopher Irion
20, 21, 22, 23, 28, 29, 43, 47, 84,
90, 100, 101, 104

David Livingston
9, 16, 17, 18, 19, 32, 34, 44, 48,
53, 56, 63, 70, 71, 76, 77, 82, 83,
86, 87, 93

Andrew McKinney
68

Jeremy Samuelson
39, 45

John Vaughan
46, 57

Alan Weintraub
10, 14, 15, 24, 25, 26, 27, 30, 35,
36, 37, 38, 49, 51, 55, 58, 59, 60,
61, 62, 69, 74, 75, 92, 98, 99, 120

ACKNOWLEDGMENTS

Warmest thanks to California's finest photographers, whose beautiful images grace these pages.
I would especially like to thank Grey Crawford for the elegant cover photo. It has also been a pleasure
working with Jeremy Samuelson, Alan Weintraub, Christopher Irion, David Livingston,
Mark Darley, David Wakely, Andrew McKinney, Thomas Heinser, and Fred Lyon.

It has been my great joy to interview California's top interior designers and chefs
concerning many aspects of this book. I am delighted to show the work of leading
California architects and kitchen designers in this book — and demonstrate the variety and quality
of design in California. I send all of the designers and talented craftspeople
my deepest gratitude. I applaud their dedication and wisdom.

Madeleine Corson's beautiful book design presents my words and
each image with clarity and grace. I thank her. Special thanks to Terry Ryan,
brilliant editor, and her trusty Black Wings.

My wonderful editor, Nion McEvoy, has enthusiastically supported my ideas
for a series of design books. To Nion, along with Christina Wilson, Christine Carswell,
Pamela Geismar, and the team at Chronicle Books, I offer sincere thanks.

With love and gratitude,
Diane Dorrans Saeks

AUTHOR

Diane Dorrans Saeks is a writer, editor, and design lecturer who specializes
in interior design, architecture, gardens, travel, and fashion. She is the California editor
for *Metropolitan Home,* a contributing editor for *Garden Design,* San Francisco correspondent
for *W* and *Women's Wear Daily,* and a frequent contributor to the *San Francisco Chronicle.*
Her articles have appeared in magazines and newspapers around the world, including
Vogue Living, Vogue Australia, In Style, the *New York Times,* the *Washington Post,*
the *Los Angeles Times,* the *London Times,* and the *Sydney Morning Herald.* She is also the
author of *California Design Library: Living Rooms* and several best-selling books on style, decor,
and design, including *California Cottages, San Francisco Interiors, San Francisco: A Certain Style*
and *California Country,* all published by Chronicle Books. She lives in San Francisco.